MW01292370

True Crime Stories

12 Shocking True
Crime Murder Cases

True Crime Anthology Vol.10

By
Jack Rosewood

DISCLAIMER:

This crime anthology biography includes quotes from those closely involved in the twelve cases examined, and it is not the author's intention to defame or intentionally hurt anyone involved. The interpretation of the events leading up to these crimes is the author's as a result of researching the true crime murders. Any comments made about the psychopathic or sociopathic behavior of criminals involved in any of these cases are the sole opinion and responsibility of the person quoted.

Free Bonus!

Get two free books when you sign
up to my VIP newsletter at
http://www.jackrosewood.com/free
150 interesting trivia about serial killers
and the story of serial killer Herbert Mullin.

Contents

Introduction

In the following pages, you will be introduced to twelve amazing crimes cases that sometimes stumped investigators and always shocked the public. Many of these cases are extremely violent and difficult to comprehend and as much as you may be so disturbed you feel like you should stop reading, you will be compelled to keep turning the pages.

These are twelve, true crime cases that are truly as fascinating as they are brutal.

In every one of these true crime anthologies, there are always one or more themes and this volume is no different. In fact, this volume contains cases that can be placed into three themes, although some of the cases overlap and can be categorized in two or all of the themes.

The most pervading theme in this volume is the scourge of youth violence and the devastation it brings to affected communities. Although, most of the youth violence cases profiled in this volume took place in the United States, youth crime and violence is certainly a world-wide problem. Numerous juvenile murderers are profiled, with not only an emphasis on the details of their crimes, but a look at what drove them to commit their antisocial acts.

You will read about how a seventeen-year-old honor student and all-around good kid named Anthony Barbaro decided one day to turn his quiet upstate New York town into a war zone. The case of the triple murder of the Doss family is also profiled. As bad as any murder is, it is always worse when it involves multiple victims, but this case was particularly perplexing when it was finally determined that the killer was a sixteen-year-old girl who was a friend of the family. You will also read about the heart-wrenching story of Robbie Middleton, an eight-year-old-boy who was attacked, set on fire, and left to die. Robbie showed incredible tenacity by surviving his horrendous wounds for several years, long enough to give a crucial piece of evidence that led to the arrest of his teen attacker.

Although the phenomenon of teen violence may dominate this volume, there are plenty of other cases with different themes. Two notable cold cases are profiled – one from the United Kingdom and the other from the United States. In the case from the United Kingdom, the murder of a woman went unsolved for decades before advances in forensic science finally led to the capture of the killer. Other than it being a cold case, the case from the United States was markedly different. The case involved the death of a little boy and how the authorities tracked his own mother nearly twenty-five years, collecting enough so that they could finally make an arrest.

Finally, as with all volumes in this series, there are a fair share of cases profiled that can only be considered bizarre.

You will read about a pair of Canadian thrill killers who took their unnatural desires for extreme sex as far as they could go, ending with the brutal murder of an innocent woman. A young Canadian serial killer is also profiled, who effectively turned many people's ideas about serial killers upside down. Finally, the tragic case of a schizophrenic who thought he was being chased by a cannibalistic cult is discussed.

So take a deep breath, brace yourself, and open the pages of this book.

CHAPTER 1:
The Cold Murder Case of Nova Welsh

Fortunately, in most industrialized countries your chances of becoming a murder victim are relatively low. True, murders happen every day and in some countries with higher crime rates they are more common, but the reality is that homicide remains among the ultimate taboos.

With that said, Hollywood and other forms of media have done their part to make it seem as if crazed killers are lurking around every corner, waiting to randomly take the life of any unsuspecting person to pass by. This mentality has led many people to arm themselves with whatever weapons are legal in their country and many more to invest in expensive home security systems.

But, the statistics show that most murders are not committed by strangers.

Although murder is uncommon, murders committed by a spouse or significant other are the most common type. For most people, it is not the crazed killer lurking in the bushes that they should be afraid of, but the person sleeping next to them in bed.

The majority of these types of murders are committed in a fit of passion and even the ones that are premeditated are done by people with little to no criminal background. Because of those factors, spousal killers are usually quickly apprehended.

Very few spousal murders become cold cases and in the few cases that are, the detectives usually know that the perpetrator is the spouse. It is just a matter of them compiling enough evidence to make an arrest that will hold up in court.

The cold murder case of Nova Welsh is unique because it is one of the few crimes of passion that went cold for decades. When Nova was murdered in 1981, the police immediately suspected her long-term boyfriend and father of her two children, but a lack of physical evidence prevented them from making an arrest. As the decades rolled by, many people forgot about the case, but a few determined investigators familiar with advances in technology were finally able to solve the case and bring closure to Nova's family.

Nova Welsh and Osmond Bell

Nova Welsh's tragic story began in the late 1950s, spanning two continents and several decades. Nova Welsh was born to a middle-class family in Jamaica during the late 1950s that wanted to find more opportunities elsewhere. Jamaica's high-crime rates, corruption, and political instability were all factors that contributed to the Welsh family looking abroad for a new start.

Although, the United States was close and is an English speaking country, its immigration laws were fairly restrictive at the time, so the Welsh's took advantage of their status as citizens in the British Commonwealth and moved to the United Kingdom.

In the period immediately following World War II, the United Kingdom began opening its doors to its former colonial subjects, which meant that thousands of Indians, Pakistanis, and Caribbean people, among others, came to the country for a number of different reasons. The desire to escape poverty in their home countries was the most pervasive reason. Jobs were more plentiful and paid more in Britain and the country had a generous safety net if one were to lose his or her job. Britain also became a safe haven for political dissidents who feared violent reprisals in their home countries.

Like most immigrants around the world, the Welsh's decided to move to a location where there were plenty of people from their old country to fall back on for support, so they chose the Midlands City of Birmingham due to its sizable West Indian/Caribbean community.

Nova was ten-years-old when the Welsh's moved to Birmingham and as difficult as the move was in some ways, it was exciting in other ways for the young Jamaican immigrant. She received a better education than she would have in Jamaica and there were far more and better material goods and creature comforts available in the United Kingdom.

But there were also unseen temptations in the new land.

Because Nova's parents worked long hours to make ends meet in the significantly more expensive United Kingdom, their supervision of Nova was relaxed. Although, Nova stayed out of trouble on Birmingham's sometimes mean streets, she came under the influence of a charismatic young Jamaican immigrant named Osmond Bell.

In the early 1970s, Osmond Bell was a familiar sight around Birmingham's Caribbean community. Bell was a smooth-talking teenager who attracted a following of other young men and boys, not to mention the attention of several girls. The young man often walked on the edge of the legal immigrant community and the underworld. Although, he never accumulated a serious criminal record, he had several contacts with Caribbean organized crime groups, which he often liked to tell people as a form of a threat.

One of those girls was Nova Welsh.

Bell was one year older than Nova, but considerably more street savvy when the two met. The young man had lived in the United Kingdom for most of his life and could move around the city of Birmingham with ease. Nova was impressed with the fact that Osmond knew people all over the city and felt safe whenever she was with him.

The two young Jamaican immigrants began a romance that

quickly became serious. Nova moved into an apartment with Osmond and by the late 1970s, the couple had two sons.

The hope and excitement that Osmond's and Nova's relationship began with was gone by the end of the decade. Bell rarely worked, was a problem drinker, and often cheated on Nova. He also refused to commit fully to the relationship by marrying Nova; but worst of all, he was physically abusive.

Bell was known to hit Nova when he got drunk or his whereabouts were questioned by her. He did his best to keep Nova isolated from her friends and family and for the first few years of their relationship he was fairly successful, but by 1981, the young mother began making some major changes in her life that didn't involve Osmond Bell.

Drifting Apart

Throughout the 1970s, Nova's sisters and friends admonished her to leave the shiftless Bell. Still, due to her traditional Caribbean roots, Nova continued to try to make the relationship work. She argued that her sons needed a father figure, but that became less and less of an issue the more Bell devolved into alcoholism and abuse.

Eventually, Nova realized that Osmond Bell would never marry her and would probably never be much of a father to their two sons, so she decided to move on with her life. She found full-time work, developed a new social network, and starting dating.

In 1981, at the age of twenty-four, Nova Welsh appeared headed in the right direction and well on her way to building a new, successful life.

Nova could no longer bear Osmond's physical and psychological abuse, so she made the assertive move of kicking him out of their apartment in July 1981. Although, he didn't like the situation, there was little he could do.

This was a new Nova Welsh.

But Osmond Bell was still in the picture.

Although, Osmond had neglected his fatherly duties by the middle of 1981, he still kept tabs on Nova. Osmond was an extremely jealous man who believed that Nova and their children were essentially his property. As he frequented the bars and shops in the Caribbean neighborhoods of Birmingham in the days after he was evicted, he learned that his children's mother was dating another man.

Osmond Bell would not stand for this.

A Crime of Passion

By early August 1981, Osmond Bell was positively outraged at the situation in which he found himself. Within a matter of weeks, he was kicked out of his apartment, lost his long-term girlfriend, and had his access to his children limited. Worst of all, it appeared that his girlfriend had moved on without him by dating another man.

Bell was persistent, though, and kept trying to get back with Nova.

Finally, on August 18, 1981, Nova Welsh relented and allowed Bell to come to her apartment to discuss their sons.

The evidence shows that Bell probably didn't go to Welsh's apartment with the intent to kill her, but instead things quickly got out of hand when Nova told him that they would never get back together.

The discussion quickly turned into an argument, which in turn led to yelling before Bell snapped, placing Nova in a choke hold, breaking her neck.

Bell was immediately faced with the reality of what he had done and that if arrested, he could face a very long prison sentence.

He had to cover his crime.

Luckily for Bell, his method of murder was relatively clean. He didn't have to worry about cleaning up blood or other bodily fluids and there was no weapon that could be tied to him. With that said, he knew that any suspicions of Nova's murder would be cast on him. Instead of leaving her body for his sons to find, he decided to hide Nova in a utility closet of the apartment complex. Bell was able to drag Nova's corpse down a flight of stairs without anyone seeing him, until he got to the utility closet that he hoped would be his ex's final resting place, at least long enough to obfuscate the police investigation.

After Bell placed Nova's body in the closet, he realized that that door didn't have a lock or even a proper latch. The broken closet door kept swinging open every time he tried to close it.

Osmond Bell was never seen as a particularly intelligent person by those who knew him, but he was resourceful. Utilizing his resourceful nature, Bell took the piece of gum he was chewing, placed it in the door jamb, and closed the closet door.

He then went on his way as if nothing happened.

Nova's body wasn't discovered until several days later when residents of the apartment complex complained about a rotten smell emanating from the little-used utility closet. When maintenance checked the source of the odor, they were shocked to find Nova Welsh's partially decomposed body.

Two Suspects

As with any homicide, the detectives immediately focused their attention on those closest to Nova who may have had reasons to kill her – Osmond Bell and her current boyfriend.

Bell and the current boyfriend were both cooperative with the police and both denied having anything to do with Nova's murder. The detectives dutifully collected all the evidence at the crime scene, but there was little they could do with the evidence based on the technology at the time. The killer left no fingerprints in the utility closet and although the prints of Bell and Nova's new boyfriend were found in her apartment, there were legitimate reasons for those being there.

The detectives next turned to investigating the backgrounds of Bell and Nova's new boyfriend. Nothing in Nova's new boyfriend's background suggested that he was violent, but the police quickly learned that Bell had a history of violence towards Nova.

Osmond Bell was looking more and more like the killer.

But, then one of Nova's friends turned a letter over to the police that she had received.

The letter claimed to have been penned by a woman who witnessed Nova's new boyfriend commit the murder. It was unsigned and the supposed writer claimed that she was too afraid to come forward publicly at that point.

The actual author of the letter was Osmond Bell, who although not especially intelligent,

was clever enough to know that such a rouse could throw the police off his trail.

Although, the detectives had a gut feeling that Bell was the killer, the letter cast doubt on that theory. There was also no physical evidence that tied Bell or the other boyfriend to the murder, so the case went cold.

Scientific Advances

As the decades went by, Osmond Bell must have surely thought he got away with murder. There were no witnesses to his crime and it seemed as though he had effectively cast enough suspicion on another person to bring the investigation to a standstill. Bell went on with his life, but as he did so, advances in science were catching up to criminal investigation procedures.

Today, the process of DNA profiling is an everyday part of police work and most people in general, know something about the procedure due to the numerous television shows, both documentary and fictional, which highlight its use in investigations. DNA profiling was first used successfully in a court case in the United Kingdom during the late 1980s and by 2016 it had been used to capture thousands of killers, rapists, and other criminals around the world.

Armed with this new technology, Birmingham homicide investigators reopened the Nova Welsh murder case by getting court orders for DNA samples from Osmond Bell and Nova Welsh's other boyfriend at the time. The samples were compared with the small amount they were able to take from the piece of gum Bell used to keep the utility closet door closed.

Bell's DNA matched that on the gum.

Osmond Bell was charged with murder in 2016 and went to trial in early 2017. Although the DNA evidence was compelling enough to place Bell at the scene of the crime, the jury didn't think he killed Welsh with premeditation. Bell was acquitted of murder but found guilty of manslaughter.

But if the Jamaican killer thought he would get off lightly, he was wrong.

When he went before the court for sentencing, he was given a verbal lashing by the judge, who found it particularly disturbing that Bell could commit such an act on the mother of his children.

"Having killed her, you concealed her body, doing nothing to assuage the pain and grief of your own children. When the police became involved, you thought it was getting a little hot. You wrote a letter intending to point suspicion away from yourself and towards someone else," said sentencing judge, Patrick Thomas.

Judge Thomas then handed down a thirty-six-year prison sentence, half of which must be served behind bars. Because Bell is now sixty-years-old, it could very well be a life sentence.

CHAPTER 2:
Michael MacGregor and Tanya Bogdanovich, the Canadian "Thrill Kill" Couple

In the annals of crime history, there are more than a few cases of killer couples. The reasons why these murderous couples killed varied to some extent, but lust was often the driving force. Usually, the man was the dominant member of the relationship and was the one who introduced the woman to the vocation of serial killing. Oftentimes, the woman was used to lure hapless female victims, although in nearly every known case, the woman also actively participated in the sadistic torture sessions and murders.

Some of the more notable killer couples include the "Sunset Strip Killers" Doug Clark and Carol Bundy, who killed seven people in 1980 in southern California. Clark is believed to have been the mastermind behind the couple's reign of terror, but Bundy was a willing participant and even committed a murder on her own.

A few hundred miles to the north of southern California, in

northern California and Nevada, married couple Gerald and Charlene Gallego, killed ten people during the late 1970s and early 1980s. Like the Sunset Strip Killers, the Gallegos were led by the male half, who meticulously planned out the details of their rapes and murders.

Less well-known to Americans, but infamous household names in Canada are Paul Bernardo and Karla Homolka. This couple was responsible for the murder of three girls and young women in Canada, including Homolka's own sister. Again, all evidence shows that it was Bernardo who planned the murders and manipulated Homolka to a certain extent.

On January 2013, another Canadian couple became almost as infamous as Bernardo and Homolka when they abducted, raped, and murdered an innocent woman. Although the couple were quickly caught, most in the law enforcement community believe that if they had not been, then they no doubt would have kept killing like the three couples mentioned in this chapter. Michael MacGregor and Tanya Bogdanovich displayed all of the anti-social hallmarks that any serial killing couple has with one major difference – the female was the dominant one in this killer couple.

Two of a Kind

At first glance, there seems to have been very few things that Michael MacGregor and Tanya Bogdanovich had in common. There was a considerable age difference and their backgrounds were very dissimilar. Still, the two shared some dark desires that eventually brought them together and later to commit murder.

Michael MacGregor was born in 1994 and grew up in the southwestern Ontario city of Sarnia. He grew up in a modest, middle-class neighborhood that was very much like one you would find across North America. Sarnia may be in the same province as Toronto, but in many ways it has a hometown feel that is more midwestern American in many ways. Crime is low, the schools are good, and people are neighborly in Sarnia, which has made it an attractive destination and a growing city.

As a child, MacGregor had no legal problems and by all accounts, was a well-adjusted kid: he got along with his neighbors and never caused problems in school. He had a good relationship with his parents and enjoyed going on trips with them.

With that said, MacGregor never could really "find himself."

He had few interests in high school, was an average student at best, and didn't have many friends. After he graduated high school, MacGregor did what most of his fellow students did and entered college, but he just wasn't ready for the rigorous studying needed to be successful at that level.

MacGregor dropped out of college during his first semester. He lived in his parents' home and for money, delivered food for a local pizzeria. For the most part, Michael MacGregor was not very different than many eighteen-year-olds, except he was missing a special someone with whom he could share his time and dreams.

But Michael MacGregor's dreams were not conventional to say the least.

When he wasn't delivering pizzas, MacGregor spent most of his free time surfing the web and visiting various internet chat rooms. He found himself drawn to websites that catered to bondage fetishes, finding that the more violent ones were the biggest turn-ons. MacGregor began downloading thousands of images of violent pornography, but he was still not satisfied – he needed to make his violent sexual fantasies a reality.

The problem was, that in the world of sexual sadism and masochism, or "S&M," he was a "sub," which means "submissive." Michael MacGregor needed to find a "dom" or "dominant" partner who could show him the way. After trying to find his dominant half on a number of websites unsuccessfully, he finally struck gold at an obscure internet chatroom named "Fetlife."

In 2012, Tanya Bogdanovich was twenty-eight-years-old and well familiar with the world of sexual sadism. Although ten years MacGregor's senior, they were a perfect fit in many ways as she was the dominant personality for which he was searching.

But they came from completely different worlds.

Where MacGregor's family life was stable and both of his parents were living at home, Bogdanovich, like many in her generation, was a child of divorce. Although countless children of divorce go on to live productive lives and some of the most notable people in modern society come from divorced families, there is no doubt that it has a negative impact on the children in such families.

Divorce clearly had a negative impact on Bogdanovich's life.

She spent most of her youth with her mother and never really knew her father, so she never received the support of a strong male figure that children need. Her mother never disciplined her much and when she did, Tanya simply ignored her. From a young age, Tanya learned that she could do virtually whatever she wanted. Her mother never really seemed to care anyway.

Bogdanovich never really seemed to fit in anywhere as a child, going from one peer group to another until she finally started to run with rougher crowds that were into drugs and alcohol. By her teen years, Bogdanovich already had a substance abuse problem and she later claimed that she was also raped as a teenager.

Like many children who are victims of sexual assault, Bogdanovich became extremely promiscuous, changing sexual partners quite frequently. Most of Bogdanovich's relationships were flawed from the beginning and many were physically and psychologically abusive. Despite the chaos that was a ubiquitous part of her life, or possibly because of it, she had three children from her late teens until her mid-twenties.

Tanya Bogdanovich never came close to winning any mother of

the year awards.

She had no job skills to speak of and since she wasn't particularly ambitious, Bogdanovich turned to the world's oldest profession to make money. Although not particularly physically attractive, Tanya Bogdonavich carved out a place for herself in the western Ontario prostitution scene by offering her services as a dominatrix.

It was through her work as a professional dominatrix that Bogdonavich was able to earn enough money to pay her rent and it also allowed her to indulge some of her more taboo desires that mixed sex and violence.

Still, she could only do so much as a professional dominatrix and the reality was that she could only do what her clients wanted – there was always a safe word that could end the session.

Bogdanovich desired something more real and more violent. For that she went to Fetlife, which is where she met MacGregor in late 2012.

Fetlife is a Canadian based website that caters to people who enjoy non-normative sexual tastes. As it states on its welcome page: "Like Facebook, but run by kinksters like you and me. We think it is more fun that way. Don't you?"

The site offers a plethora of different chatrooms and a message board where "kinksters" can discuss their sexual fetishes with like-minded people or possibly find a sexual partner.

The site, though, has been the source of controversy.

Besides its obvious content that is enough to make many people cringe, Fetlife users have been involved in more than one criminal investigation. Most recently, Illinoisan, Brendt Christensen, was charged with kidnapping a female Chinese scholar named Yingying Zhang in June 2017 near the University of Illinois campus in Urbana, Illinois. The investigation has revealed that Christensen had a kidnapping and rape fetish and that he was quite open about it on numerous message boards dedicated to similar fetishes on Fetlife.

Bogdanovich and MacGregor met on a message board dedicated to bondage and sadism fetishes.

Sexually speaking, the two were a perfect fit. MacGregor was a "sub" and Bogdanovich was a "dom."

The two spent several hours online discussing their sexual preferences and fantasies, which besides S&M, also included rape fantasies. After simulating their fantasies in chatrooms and then on their phones, the two decided to take their relationship to the real world.

But when the couple did take their fantasies into real life, they both felt that they had to go as far as they could with it. The pair's idea of S&M was on the extreme side when considered among that of other aficionados of the fetish.

For instance, to Bogdanovich and MacGregor, simply tying each other up with bedsheets was not enough. Instead, they role-played violent rape scenarios where choking and cutting with knives was the norm. The two especially like to choke each other until the point of passing out. They found it thrilling to see their partner's eyes roll back into their head as they were about to lose consciousness. The knife play could also get serious as there was more than one occasion where injuries were sustained.

For MacGregor, the transition of their relationship from the virtual to the real world was a dream come true. The socially awkward college drop-out now had a girlfriend who shared his same dark desires. He had a lot to look forward to in late 2012.

For Bogdanovich, it was just another notch in her belt of sexual conquests.

Tanya was actually involved in a long-term relationship with another man when she began her real-world sexual relationship with MacGregor, but that mattered little to the mother of three. Bogdanovich operated under the premise that everything and everyone in the world was there to fulfill her needs or entertain her in some way. Tanya was also attracted to weaker men, so her current boyfriend had little say, concerning what she did with other men.

MacGregor, though, seemed perfect for Bogdanovich.

"I feel so lucky, I can't even believe it. I can feed every need. I can fulfill every urge, I feel no shame about what I like or who I am with you because U (sic) have the (sic) urges or at least ones that work so perfectly with mine," Bogdanovich said to MacGregor in an instant message.

But a relationship built on S&M and rape fantasy fetishes can only last so long.

Eventually, the two began to tire of the situation; MacGregor began seeing other women and Bogdanovich also kept her revolving door of men working. But just when it seemed that their demented relationship would end, Bogdanovich posted an eerie message online to her favorite "sub."

"Rape brought us together, violence has kept us together, violence has kept us going and rape will be what holds us strong when our bond is challenged."

In order to keep her "sub" happy, Bogdanovich formulated some sick ideas that involved abduction, rape, and eventually murder.

A Diabolical Plot

The violent kidnapping, rape, and murder fantasies that MacGregor and Bogdanovich acted out and eventually turned into reality were disturbing enough on there own, but they are even more so when one considers that Bogdanovich was not only a mother of three children at the time but also a nurse.

When Tanya was working as a prostitute and dominatrix, she went to nursing school in her spare time. It may seem strange that someone so broken and dysfunctional, who reveled in causing and receiving pain, would enter a profession where she would help alleviate people's pain. Perhaps she thought the work would be easy, or maybe she thought she could get her hands on some prescription drugs to use in one of her fantasies, whatever the reason, she took the Hippocratic Oath and went into nursing.

Although, she was not the brightest student, Bogdanovich eventually completed her schooling and found work full-time as a nurse in the Sarnia area.

If only her employers knew what she was really like.

By early December 2012, Bogdanovich told her willing sexual acolyte that they needed to make their violent sexual fantasies reality and in order to do so, they obviously had to find a victim. Since neither of the two were seasoned criminals, their early plans were full of holes and the attempts to carry them out were awkward at best.

But they both knew that they wanted a young female victim.

The couple decided to go on "dry runs" at the local Sarnia mall where they would approach teenage girls and ask them if they would like to leave with them and go somewhere else. After a few dry runs, the pair thought better of the plan when they realized that malls are full of witnesses and security cameras.

The next evil idea came straight from the mind of Tanya Bogdanovich.

Bogdanovich thought she would really surprise her boyfriend with something appropriate and original for his nineteenth birthday. Instead of giving him an electronic device or some clothes, Tanya gave MacGregor a collection of digital images comprised of local teenage girls she took from Facebook profiles.

MacGregor was ecstatic.

The couple spent hours looking through the images and gathering information on their favorite girls in order to decide the best time and place to snatch their quarry. They stalked the local mall and area high schools looking for their favorite victim. The couple also practiced their roles in the kidnapping numerous times on each other.

But despite all the time the couple put into finding a victim for their twisted sexual fantasies, their crime ended up being one of opportunity.

New Year's Eve 2012 was a big night in Sarnia. The bars were filled with revelers and just as many people were attending New Year's house parties, which is where twenty-seven-year-old Noelle Paquette found herself.

Paquette was an attractive school teacher who never had a problem making new friends. According to her friends and family, her smile was infectious and she was the type of person who would give you the shirt off her back if needed. She was also extremely trusting of people.

Too trusting.

The night had not gone the way Paquette had planned. Instead of spending some quality time with her boyfriend, the two ended up at a loud party where both had drank too much and then got into an argument. Noelle pleaded with her boyfriend to leave the party, but he said he was enjoying himself and wanted to stay. A couple of hours after the new year of 2013, Noelle had enough and told her boyfriend that she was walking home.

The last text message that Noelle sent was around 2:30 am on January 1, 2013, to her boyfriend.

New Year's Eve was a particularly boring night for Tanya Bogdanovich. She spent the night working until 11 pm and then ran some errands and drove around Sarnia extensively. Sometime after 2:30 am, she noticed the attractive Paquette walking alone down the cold streets of Sarnia underdressed.

Bogdanovich pulled up next to Paquette and offered her a ride. The school teacher at first declined the offer, but reconsidered when she thought about how long she had to walk in the cold. She was also reassured by Bogdanovich's demeanor. The sexual sadist could appear sweet and even charming if need be.

Once Paquette got into Bogdanovich's car, the two drove a short distance until they pulled over to let a man into the car.

It was Michael MacGregor.

Bogdanovich had texted her paramour to alert him of the situation and that it looked like they would finally turn their violent fantasies into reality.

MacGregor got into the backseat behind Paquette and pulled out a knife and put it to the young woman's neck. He told her that if she would cooperate then she'd live.

MacGregor and Bogdanovich had no intention of letting Paquette go. They agreed ahead of time to leave no witnesses and not only that, the act of murder would fuel their sexual highs.

Without saying a word, Bogdanovich drove to a location about fifteen miles outside of Sarnia the couple had reconnoitered recently. MacGregor dragged the frightened, crying Paquette from the car and threw her to the cold, hard ground.

As Noelle begged for her life, the despicable duo merely laughed as MacGregor handed the knife to Bogdanovich. The young sadist then proceeded to rape the school teacher. But Noelle's torment had just begun – the duo then took turns stabbing her for a total of forty-nine times.

After killing Paquette, the two lovers shared a passionate embrace and then left the scene.

Not far from the murder scene, Bogdanovich and MacGregor were pulled over for a minor traffic violation. The police noticed that the duo was covered in blood and that blood was all over the car's interior. A further search revealed that MacGregor was bleeding from an injury. Perplexed at the situation, the police asked where all the blood came from, which Bogdanovich answered that they were engaged in S&M in the woods and were celebrating the New Year "with kink."

The police were rightfully suspicious, but Paquette's body had yet to be found, so MacGregor was brought to the local hospital for his wounds and Bogdanovich was able to leave.

No Way Out

As MacGregor was being put on a stretcher for the ambulance ride to the hospital, he made the curious remark "is this the strangest thing you ever had?" to one of the paramedics. The paramedic told the police officers at the scene about the question, who then gave their "accident" victim more scrutiny. MacGregor went into surgery for his wounds, which looked like self-inflicted stab wounds to the attending physicians.

The suspicions surrounding the circumstances of MacGregor's admittance to the hospital were aggravated by Tanya Bogdanovich, who spent most of January 1st and 2nd lurking around the hospital's ER waiting room. Many of the hospital staff thought she was acting extremely strange and others believed that she was MacGregor's mother.

Bogdanovich's concern for MacGregor's condition probably had less to do with worries about his health, than it did about what he might say about their thrill kill of Noelle Paquette. Tanya may have enjoyed her twisted time with MacGregor, but it was becoming apparent that she didn't trust him.

Noelle Paquette's mangled body was finally found on January 2nd and at that point, it was only a matter of time before the police determined that Bogdanovich and MacGregor were the culprits. Less than thirty hours after the discovery of Noelle Paquette's body, Bogdanovich was arrested outside of the hospital and MacGregor was taken at a nearby motel.

Once the two were in police custody, they spilled their guts. Neither offered much of a defense, which is why the people of the city of Sarnia and the province of Ontario were not surprised when the murderous duo pleaded guilty in February 2016 to Paquette's murder. MacGregor's lawyer later said that his client's plea was done to spare his and Paquette's family the pain of a trial, but the reality is that he was perhaps the most hated person in Canada at the time and there was no way he could have beaten the charges.

There was no legal way out of the situation for either MacGregor or Bogdanovich.

When the two were sentenced, the judge gave an especially sharp rebuke of their lives and actions.

"You chose in the darkest and most violent way to satisfy your overpowering lust," said Superior Court Justice Bruce Thomas. "Your actions are vile and they are despicable and as a result, you will be removed from the society for what might perhaps be for the rest of your lives."

CHAPTER 3:
The Murder of Timothy Wiltsey

It is said that murder is the ultimate taboo, so therefore, the most taboo of all murders would be the killing of a child. The reason should be obvious to most: children are innocent. Children have yet to make the mistakes in life that often put adults in positions to be killed. While random murders such as the murder of Noelle Paquette do occur, they are the exception and not the rule. Most murder victims are acquainted with their killers and the situation in which the murders take place are often more complicated and nuanced than what is reported on the local ten o'clock news.

But things are much different when a child is murdered.

The abduction and murder of a child is something that cannot be justified and most find it impossible to forgive a person who does such a thing. Although, many seem to believe that these types of murders are committed almost entirely by strangers, the reality is that vindictive parents are just as likely to commit such a heinous crime. The idea that a parent could somehow abduct and kill his or her own child, is something that is truly difficult for most people to grasp – it becomes nearly impossible to do so when it is revealed that the killer is the child's mother.

The overwhelming number of mothers in the world have a maternal instinct to provide for and protect their children. Human mothers are often compared to female bears, which would do anything to protect their cubs. Since the Paleolithic era, when humans still lived in caves, it was the mothers who spent most of the time with their children and who were the child's last line of defense if the men were not around or had been captured or killed. Even today, the instinct that mother's have to protect their children is still very much alive. One does not have to peruse the Internet very long to find news stories of protective mothers who foiled home invasions or who helped capture a sex offender.

Unfortunately, there are mothers who have no maternal instinct.

Michelle Lodzinski is one such woman who was apparently born with no maternal instinct. In 1991, in a case that can only be described as bizarre, Lodzinski stood accused of abducting and murdering her own five-year-old son, Timothy Wiltsey. The struggle to bring Wiltsey's killer to justice spanned several thousands of miles and numerous states over a period of nearly twenty-five years.

But when the judge's gavel finally came down, it seemed there were still more questions than answers surrounding the case.

Michelle Lodzinski

Lodzinski was born the youngest of six children from a strong Roman Catholic family in northern New Jersey in 1968. Although, young Michelle may not have gotten all of the luxury items she wanted as a child due to the size of her family, her father was a good provider. The Lodzinski children always had enough food to eat and they always had clean clothes.

The Lodzinski children were brought up in the Church and all were required to take the sacraments; but as Michelle became a teenager... things changed.

Lodzinski's friends and family reported that the changes in Michelle were not drastic, but that she was more interested in hanging out with her older boyfriend, George Wiltsey, than she was in going to church or spending time with her family. Eventually, Witlsey convinced Michelle to move with him to Iowa where he had family who could help him find work. Although Michelle's parents were initially against the move, when they learned that Michelle was pregnant, they gave their blessing.

Michelle was depressed during her sojourn in Iowa, which is not extraordinary when one considers all of the circumstances. She was still very young, a juvenile by legal standards, and therefore probably frightened and concerned about what the future held for her. Along with that, all of her friends and family, her support network were over 1,000 miles away in New Jersey.

Then there was the weather.

Although New Jersey gets its fair share of snow and cold temperatures in the winter, it is nothing compared to Iowa, where due to its location in the middle of the continent, the weather can change quite rapidly in a matter of hours. Not only that, but winter can last for six months in the Hawkeye state.

The separation from her family and the cold Iowa winter proved to be too much for Lodzinski.

One day, not long after Timothy was born, Lodzinski packed everything up and moved back to New Jersey with her newborn son. George later claimed that he was not happy, but did little to fight the move. Michelle never filed for child support and sent back every present that George attempted to send to his son.

Michelle Lodzinski simply erased that part of her life.

Lodzinski seemed to have a talent for simply walking away from and erasing parts of her life that she didn't like. After leaving George Wiltsey, she would repeat the pattern with other men, jobs, and ultimately her own son.

After leaving her son's father behind in Iowa, Lodzinski had no problems meeting men in New Jersey. Michelle was a fairly attractive young woman, had a good personality, and was always looking for a man who could take care of her. She had no problem meeting men, but few usually called her back for a second date. She later claimed that none of the men she dated wanted a relationship with her when they learned about Timothy.

Lodzinski may have had relationship problems during the late 1980s and early 1990s, but she did have her immediate family to support her and Timothy. By all accounts, the Lodzinski family was very supportive by helping Michelle watch Timothy when she was at work and by offering money when times were tough.

And times could get tough for Michelle.

Lodzinski dropped out of high school to have Timothy and although she later earned her General Equivalency Degree, it did little more than help her get entry-level jobs with few prospects for advancement. Lodzinski's good looks and personality were often enough to get her jobs in offices and banks, but she often grew bored of these positions and routinely quit before finding another job.

Still, the money Lodzinski made in entry-level office jobs, combined with funds from her family meant that she could send Timothy to a private Catholic school in South Amboy, New Jersey. By the middle of 1991, Lodzinski was working as a bank teller and everything seemed to be going well for her. Timothy liked his school and she seemed to be at peace with life.

But sometimes looks can be deceiving.

Timothy's Disappearance

Memorial Day weekend 1991 was a particularly warm one in northern New Jersey. Those who weren't indoors enjoying their air conditioning were either at the beach or at one of the many outdoor carnivals taking place around the state. Michelle Lodzinski told friends and family that she planned to take Timothy to a nearby carnival in Sayreville, New Jersey that weekend to celebrate the end of the school year and the beginning of summer.

Lodzinski's neighbors reported seeing Timothy playing in his front yard on the afternoon of May 25th , which happened to be the last day he was seen alive.

Later that evening, a distressed Lodzinski reported that Timothy had gone missing from the Sayreville carnival. She claimed that they were waiting in line for a ride, but that she left him for a few minutes to buy some soft drinks. When she returned to their place in line, Timothy was gone.

Although taking place more than ten years before the Amber Alert system was implemented in the United States, the disappearance of Timothy Wiltsey quickly grabbed headlines. The case was featured in local media, which included the nearby New York City market, before getting picked up by national news outlets. John Walsh featured the case on his *America's Most Wanted* television show and Timothy's picture was displayed on milk cartons throughout the northeast. As the media attention picked up, more and more attention was being given to Michelle Lodzinski.

And Lodzinski was not afraid of the attention.

The story that she told to the police and the media began to be seen as strange and suspicious by most people. Reporters questioned why she would leave a five-year-old alone in line, which she answered by simply saying, "He doesn't like to wait in lines."

The general public also was surprised and disturbed to a certain extent at how little emotion Lodzinski seemed to show. She always answered questions about her son's disappearance matter-of-factly with a flat affect and never cried. When asked about this, she replied:

"Everyone is waiting to see a grieving mother on TV break down, crying, hysterical because the public, they thrive on that stuff," Lodzinski told reporters in 1991. "But I'm not going to do it."

As Lodzinski was giving her emotionless interviews to the press, the public weren't the only ones watching. The local police were beginning to think that the young mother knew more than what she was saying about her son's disappearance.

Lodzinski was interviewed numerous times by the local police and each time her story seemed to change. She told the investigators that before going to the carnival, she and Tim visited a local park. The investigators later learned that the park was closed that day.

She then told the detectives that Timothy was wearing a bright red shirt that day, which would have been memorable, but no one at the carnival remembered seeing him. In fact, the only people other than Lodzinski who remembered seeing Timothy on May 25th were the next door neighbors.

Eventually, the detectives called Lodzinski on her obvious lies and duplicity, which caused her to change her story yet again. She then claimed that two men with a knife abducted Timothy and in another interview she said that two men and a stripper named "Ellen" took her son. Lodzinski offered no reason why someone who she knew would take her son or why she failed to call the police immediately after it happened.

At this point, the police asked Lodzinski to take a polygraph test.

Although polygraph tests, often known as "lie detectors," are not admissible in any criminal court proceedings in the United States, police routinely use them to eliminate people from their suspect pools. Results from a polygraph examination can also be used to get search warrants.

For whatever reason, most likely arrogance, Lodzinski agreed to take the test.

She failed miserably.

After Lodzinski failed the polygraph test, the results were leaked to the press and what little public support Michelle once had quickly evaporated. Out of desperation, she agreed to take another polygraph exam.

During the exam, Lodzinski even asked "how am I doing?" The

examiner didn't need to respond – she failed the second exam as badly as the first.

Despite everything seeming to point toward Michelle Lodzinski either being involved in her own son's disappearance, or at least knowing much more about it than she was telling the police, there was not enough evidence to make an arrest. In fact, since there was no body, the police didn't even know what crime was committed, if in fact a crime was committed at all.

As the months after Timothy's disappearance rolled by, the case receded a bit from the public eye. Other stories were being covered in the local media, which led some to believe that Michelle Lodzinski was getting away with something awful.

Then the case took a major turn on October 26, 1991.

On that afternoon, a schoolteacher named Daniel O'Malley was indulging in his favorite pastime of birdwatching. The urban sprawl of New York City, which most of northern New Jersey is a part of, may not seem like a good place to watch birds, but the state is full of many swamps and sloughs that are located between and among office parks and housing developments. The wooded areas are great places to watch birds and also to hide bodies.

On the day in question, as O'Malley was searching for birds, he found a children's "Teenage Mutant Ninja Turtles" themed tennis shoe. At first he thought nothing of the discovery, but the more he thought about it he realized that something just didn't fit.

Then he remembered the disappearance of Timothy Wiltsey.

O'Malley specifically remembered Michelle Lodzinski telling reporters that Timothy was wearing Teenage Mutant Ninja Turtles themed shoes when he went missing. Knowing that the find could be important, O'Malley brought the shoe to the Sayreville Police Department.

With their suspicions already firmly fixed on Lodzinski, Sayreville investigators called Michelle in order to identify the shoe as Timothy's. Interestingly, or perhaps not so, Lodzinski was adamant that the shoe did not belong to her missing son.

After Lodzinski's denials, the police promptly sent the shoe to the lab for forensic testing. Unfortunately, forensic testing in 1991 was far from where it is today. DNA profiling was a new procedure that was not used in every case and when it was, it was very expensive and time-consuming. Since Timothy was a minor, though, extra manpower and resources were dedicated to testing the shoe, which resulted as inconclusive.

Despite the setback, the local police believed that the shoe's location was the key to finding Timothy. After the shoe was found, the FBI also began assisting local and state law enforcement in the investigation.

The winter months prohibited investigators from returning to the area where O'Malley found the children's shoe, but when Spring arrived FBI agents canvassed the area, eventually discovering Timothy Wiltsey's skeletal remains on April 23rd and 24th , 1992.

Now investigators knew that Timothy was murdered after he was abducted.

Gathering Evidence against Lodzinski

By the middle of 1992, the local police and FBI had only one suspect in Timothy Wiltsey's abduction and murder – Michelle Lodzinski. Homicide detectives and FBI agents combined their resources in a task force to compile as much evidence as they could find against Lodzinski and then make an arrest.

But they found making an arrest was not so easy.

The circumstantial evidence against Lodzinski seemed convincing enough to most in law enforcement. Lodzinski's story about the fair just didn't add up as no one remembered seeing Timothy there with his mother.

"I got a sick feeling," said Laura Mechkowski about her encounter with Lodzinski at the carnival. "I spoke with her and she did not have a child with her. I was very upset. There was a child missing and there was no child."

As damning as statements from eyewitnesses at the carnival may have been, the discovery of Timothy's body proved to be even harder for Lodzinski to explain. Not only had she once worked at a nearby office park, but she failed to disclose that information to the FBI.

Still, there was not enough for the authorities to make an arrest.

But that didn't mean that they couldn't apply pressure to Lodzinski.

Homicide detectives and FBI agents made routine calls and visits to nearly all of Lodzinski's friends and family, which started to take a toll on the former mother mentally. By late 1993, Lodzinski seemed obsessed with the FBI as she talked about their surveillance of her constantly and developed a paranoia of the law enforcement organization that was not totally without merit.

Then came January 21, 1994.

On that day, a family member of Lodzinski's found her car mysteriously idling outside of her home with no one inside it. More family members soon arrived at the house to look for Lodzinski, but she was nowhere to be found.

It seemed that Michelle Lodzinski had just vanished off the face of the earth.

To her friends and family that believed her innocence, the new turn of events seemed to validate her claims that Timothy was abducted by shady thugs. To them, it appeared that she had also met the same fate. The Lodzinskis sat by their phones and searched around northern New Jersey for three days when they received the call that Michelle was found hundreds of miles away in downtown Detroit.

Lodzinski's family and friends were at a loss as to why she was in

Detroit. She had no family or friends there, so it must be connected to the people who abducted and murdered Timothy they reasoned. But when Michelle returned to New Jersey, things got even more bizarre.

Lodzinski claimed that the FBI abducted her and for whatever reason, dropped her off in Detroit three days later. She never gave a specific reason why the FBI would do such a thing and only talked vaguely about conspiracies against her. Two weeks after the incident, Michelle's brother received a threatening message written on an FBI business card. It was at this point when Michelle Lodzinski began losing the few supporters she had left. People began to think that Lodzinski was either crazy, trying to shift the guilt in her son's murder, or both.

No one believed that an FBI agent would send a threatening note on his own business card.

The FBI later located the print shop where the card was made and confirmed that Michelle Lodzinski was the person who ordered the custom-made card.

Although investigators were slowly amassing a pile of circumstantial evidence against Lodzinski, she remained free to live her life. By the late 1990s, it seemed as though Lodzinski had moved on with her life and never expected to hear from investigators again.

At least in regards to the murder of Timothy.

Lodzinski was arrested for stealing a computer from her place of employment in 1997, which led to her moving from New Jersey to Florida. After living in Florida briefly, she moved to Minnesota and then back to Florida in 2003. Lodzinski had married and given birth to another child: life seemed to be treating her fine by the early 2000s.

But the homicide investigators working on Timothy's case never gave up.

An Arrest

The primary reason why Michelle Lodzinski was not arrested in the 1990s, despite the immense amount of circumstantial evidence that pointed toward her guilt, was that there was a lack of physical evidence. The police could have arrested her at any time, but county prosecutors told the police that the charges probably would not stick even if a grand jury indicted Lodzinski. They were repeatedly told that the public was becoming more tech savvy and were aware of advances in forensic technology.

The police needed to find a forensic "smoking gun."

A smoking gun was never found, but enough circumstantial evidence was uncovered to make an arrest. Perhaps the best evidence the authorities had was a blue blanket in which Timothy's remains were wrapped. Numerous witnesses stated that it looked like the exact same blanket that Lodzinski tucked Timothy into bed with every night.

Finally, in 2014, Middlesex County New Jersey prosecutors believed that the investigators had collected enough evidence to not only charge Michelle Lodzinski with her son's murder, but also to convict her.

New Jersey authorities traveled to sunny Florida where they arrested the unsuspecting Lodzinski and later formally extradited her to New Jersey. In a trial that most considered a foregone conclusion, but was no less heart wrenching, Lodzinski was found guilty of murder in May 2016. She was sentenced to a minimum of thirty years in prison in January 2017.

Michelle Lodzinski evaded justice for nearly a quarter of a century, but will now more than likely die behind bars for committing the ultimate taboo.

CHAPTER 4:
The James Franklin Murder Spree

The phenomenon of family annihilation has been covered numerous times throughout the volumes of this true crime series. It is a special type of mass murder that seems much worse than other types of mass murders. Mass murders committed on the job are often barely thought about and have even become the source of macabre jokes – the term "going postal," which generally refers to someone losing his or her cool is derived from a series of mass shootings at U.S. post offices during the 1980s and 1990s. Although the vast majority of us never consider homicide as a viable alternative to real-world problems, we've all had problems at work and can therefore understand, on some level, why a person would shoot up his or her workplace.

But it is nearly impossible to understand why someone would kill his entire family.

Although family annihilations are rare, they are the most common form of mass murder in the United States. Family annihilations affect the psyche of the general public so much, that some of the more notable cases have made it into pop culture.

The 1974 annihilation of the DeFeo family in Long Island, New York by Ronald DeFeo Junior left both parents and all four of Ronald Junior's siblings dead. Although the motives for the murders were probably financially and drug based, the sheer violence of the acts led to the creation of the *Amityville Horror* franchise of books and movies.

The 1988 Brom family murders near Rochester, Minnesota, is another example of a family annihilation that shocked the public that its details made it into pop culture. In that case, the Brom's sixteen-year-old son, David, killed both of his parents and two siblings with an axe. In the years since the Brom murders, the Chicago based heavy metal band Macabre has retold the gory story in a song recorded on one of their albums and in live performances to their legions of fans.

On the night of March 10, 1998, a teenager named Jeffrey Franklin attempted to take his place alongside Ronald DeFeo Junior and David Brom as the most notorious, and youngest, of family annihilators. Franklin brought death and destruction to his quiet Huntsville, Alabama neighborhood that night, but thankfully came up short in his kill count and his bid to become an official family annihilator.

The Franklin Family

At first glance, the Franklins seemed like a quintessential all-American family. Father Gerald and mother Cynthia worked hard to build an upper-middle-class life for themselves and their four children. They were raised in traditional southern families themselves and wanted to pass on many of their beliefs and traditions to their children, especially their belief in Christianity. Gerald and Cynthia were involved in their children's school functions and promoted a Christian lifestyle at all times, which meant that swearing was not allowed in the home, attendance at church was required, and the children were monitored.

Of course, the way children turn out in these types of homes varies. Most end up like their parents, but in some ways the heavy emphasis on rules make it ripe for rebellion. By the time he reached his teens, oldest son Jeffrey seemed to do whatever he could to test his parents' patience, but to those who knew the Franklins, there was always something more to Jeff's rebellion. Something they just couldn't put their fingers on.

Something just wasn't right with Jeffrey.

Jeffrey's parents began noticing small things about their son at an early age that seemed a little "off." He would pull pranks on other kids and his family, which often landed him in trouble with his teachers and parents. It was mostly small things like talking back to teachers or moving desks around in the classroom. Although Jeffrey never did anything violent or too serious, his parents were concerned enough to bring him to a youth behavioral specialist.

After a plethora of examinations, doctors diagnosed Jeffrey with attention deficit hyperactivity disorder. The Franklins were a bit upset to learn that their son was afflicted with a disease, but they were also thankful that it was fairly common and treatable. Jeffrey was prescribed the drug Ritalin and everything seemed to be fine.

Then Jeffrey became a teenager.

When Jeffrey entered his teen years, he began hanging around what his parents thought was a tough crowd. They all wore black and identified with the "gothic" subculture that was popular during the 1990s. Jeffrey quickly adopted the look, music, and lingo as he began using words and phrases that his parents didn't quite understand.

Nor did they want to understand.

Still, Jeffrey continued to attend church with his parents and looked to be on his way to graduating high school on time and then going on to college. His parents hoped that the goth phase would pass once he went on to college and developed new interests and friends. But by early 1998, Jeffrey Franklin was digging himself into a very deep and dark hole.

The gothic clothing and music may have seemed disturbing to Jeffrey's parents and siblings, but the real problems were developing during his extracurricular activities. By early 1998, Jeffrey had quit all official extracurricular activities at his school and instead opted to spend most of his free time drinking and doing illicit drugs. There is evidence that his parents learned of his extensive partying and tried to put an end to it, but Jeffrey was not going to let anyone tell him what to do.

He would kill if necessary.

The Attacks

The precise reasons why Jeffrey Franklin turned his wrath on his own family are still unclear. Again, it is nearly impossible for most people to even consider such a thing, but it appears that Jeffrey had been quarreling with his parents for some time over his alcohol and drug use before the events of March 10, 1998.

Based on Franklin's statements to the police and a handwritten note he wrote earlier detailing the plan, a chronology of the event can be made.

Apparently no one in the Franklin family knew what Jeffrey had in store for them that evening. There were no arguments beforehand nor did Jeffrey make any threats. He simply started attacking his family members.

Jeffrey attacked his mother first with an interesting weapon. Instead of starting the massacre out with a more traditional weapon such as a knife, gun, or club, Jeffrey attacked his mother with a flat or rat-tail file. Although the tool's killing efficiency is probably questionable, Jeff got the jump on his mom and quickly killed her by hitting, stabbing, and gouging her with the file.

After committing the act of matricide, Jeffrey then searched for his fourteen-year-old sister who he found in another part of the house. He struck his sister numerous times with a hatchet, but miraculously she lived.

The next three members of the Franklin family were attacked in quick succession.

Once he realized his mother was dead, Jeffrey changed weapons to a sledgehammer. Although the sledgehammer was much heavier, Jeffrey used his stealth tactics once more by surprising his father when he came in the front door. Jeff bashed his dad in the head a few times with the hammer and then switched back to the hatchet.

It was time to kill his nine and six-year-old brothers.

By the time he got to his brothers, they had heard enough of the commotion throughout the house to know they needed to get out. Jeffrey managed to inflict some wounds on the two kids, but they were aware enough to play dead.

Jeffrey's dad Gerald was still alive, though, and he managed to make it out of the back door of the home before he collapsed and eventually died. A neighbor saw Gerald fleeing from the back of his home, bleeding, and called the police.

When the police arrived at the Franklin home, Jeffrey made one last desperate attempt to stay free by fleeing in his car with the cops giving chase. Apparently knowing that his situation was untenable, Jeffrey pulled his car over and gave up. As he was driven away handcuffed by the Huntsville police, he turned in the backseat of the police car and stuck his tongue out for all the news cameras.

The Aftermath

When the final kill count was tallied, Jeffrey Franklin fell short of his infamous family annihilating peers. He managed to kill both his parents, but his three siblings survived with varying degrees of injuries. Generally speaking, three murders are needed for instance to be considered a "mass murder" and since most of his family lived, it cannot be considered a true family annihilation.

Despite Jeffrey's failure to attain mass murdering infamy, the attacks left an indelible mark on the community of Huntsville.

The homicide investigators assigned to the case were surprised and appalled at the level of brutality that Jeff inflicted on his family. The city has its share of crime, but most of it is drug or gang related and the domestic violence that happens never approaches the levels Jeff Franklin dished out to his family that night.

Blood was sprayed on walls and pooled on the floors.

As the investigators worked their way through the house, room by room, they made an interesting discovery in Jeff's room. Shoved far inside of a stereo speaker was a note that can only be described as Jeffrey's blueprint for murder.

"I know Dad will be home at this time and I'm going to be, I'll wait by the front door, behind the little hutch, and I'll hit him with a hammer. Mom will be out on a walk, when she comes back I'll have the radio playing loudly, I'll call Mom in the room and ask her what's on the agenda for today, then I'll kill her, and what about the brothers and sisters. Well, I'll take them, I'll strangle my little brother in this room and I'll lure my other little brother into this room and strangle him. Then my sister I will rape her then I will finish her off."

As graphic as the note was, it never related *why* Jeffrey wanted to kill his family. Still, it proved intent, which is what prosecutors would need to secure a first-degree murder conviction against Jeffrey Franklin.

Alabama is considered a "law and order" state because it has the death penalty, which it regularly uses, and criminals are routinely given long sentences. The district attorney pushed hard to give Franklin the death penalty and the conservative citizens of Madison County, Alabama appeared willing to give it to the juvenile.

Seeing that he had no defense and that a guilty verdict might mean a trip to Alabama's death row, Franklin pleaded guilty to murder and was sentenced to three consecutive life sentences.

It appeared that Franklin would spend the rest of his life in prison.

For many serial killers and mass murderers who are captured, prison is a difficult experience. These people often seem scary to normal people and they no doubt are scary when one considers their horrendous acts, but when they are placed in an environment of equity with other criminals, they tend to be on the bottom of the prison totem pole. They are routinely reviled and abused by the seasoned inmates, who are often career criminals and/or gang members.

When Jeffrey Franklin entered the Alabama Department of Corrections, he soon learned that he was on the bottom of the totem pole.

Since his incarceration, Franklin has received numerous misconduct reports, one for attempting to cut his wrists and another for slamming his head into a wall. From what little has leaked out of the prison system concerning Franklin's life in there, it appears that he has been the target of abuse by other inmates and was once beaten severely by another inmate.

Still, prison is a place where inmates have a lot of time on their hands. They use the free time to better themselves, prey on other inmates, and to devise ways to get out, both legal and illegal. Jeffrey Franklin has used much of his free time in prison to free himself legally. It turns out that Alabama inmates with life sentences can apply for parole after serving fifteen years.

Franklin argued that with time served in the county jail while he was awaiting trial, he was eligible to apply for parole in 2013. Although the courts did add the county jail time to his prison sentence, he was not given a parole hearing until the summer of 2016.

Franklin was denied.

Franklin's parole denial, though, is largely a moot point as Madison County prosecutor Rob Broussard explained.

"Number one, if you have three consecutive life sentences, I would think he's not eligible for a serious look to parole unless he's done three consecutive life sentences, 45 years," Broussard said. "I think when you look at the nature of the crime, him killing his parents in the way he killed them. And on top of that, an individual who tried to kill his three siblings, including a six-year-old with a butcher knife, this guy will always be inherently dangerous and I feel confident that a parole board will not let him see the light of day."

When Jeffrey Franklin is not being abused by the stronger inmates, he spends his time painting and drawing, which has finally given him a bit of the notoriety. Thanks to the website deathmerchant.com, Franklin has been able to reach out to a host of serial killer and mass murderer groupies. He has also been able to sell some of his artwork on the website. Because of the website, Franklin has developed a modest following of his own groupies, which although he technically failed as a family annihilator, he has finally achieved a certain level of infamy to put him on par with the likes of Defeo Junior and Brom.

Thanks to the computer age, it appears that we may not have heard the last of Jeffrey Franklin.

CHAPTER 5:

The Anthony Barbaro School Shooting

Family annihilations may account for the most deaths in mass murders in the United States, but school shootings have received much more attention. The phenomenon of mass murders committed by civilians during peacetime is actually very new. There were few such cases reported before the 1960s, but after that time they have unfortunately become much more frequent.

Mass murders can happen anywhere – a mall, a workplace, on the street – but when they happen at a school it is especially shocking. Most people value the concept of schools and view them with an almost reverent attitude – schools are the institutions that teach our children and young people how to be good, productive citizens in society.

An assault on a school is an assault on all of us.

For most of American history, schools have been viewed as peaceful places devoid of violence for the most part. Yes, schoolyard fights are fairly common among boys, but those fights are usually minor and resolved very quickly. Americans have traditionally felt safe in schools – until August 1, 1966.

That was the date when a University of Texas graduate student named Charles Whitman opened fire on students, faculty, and others from a tower on the University of Texas' main campus in Austin. Whitman's mass shooting left seventeen people dead, including himself, and rocked the United States.

From that point on, Americans looked at schools much differently.

A series of other school shootings followed Whitman's rampage. On January 17, 1989, a man named Patrick Purdy opened fire on a Stockton, California elementary school killing six. The most infamous mass murder of the 1990s took place on April 20, 1999, when teenagers Eric Harris and Dylan Klebold shot up their high school, killing fifteen people including themselves. Finally, the worst school massacre in American history happened on the campus of Virginia Tech University when former student Seung-Hui Cho shot and killed thirty-two students and employees of the college on April 16, 2007.

There are of course other school shootings, but those are the best known and worst in terms of kill counts.

But before Purdy shot up a playground full of pre-teens and after Whitman brought chaos to Austin, a teenager named Anthony Barbaro decided to shoot up his upstate New York high school on December 30, 1974. Barbaro's massacre is often overlooked because he did not deliver as much carnage as the others – he killed three and wounded eleven – and it took place nearly ten years after Whitman's massacre and more than ten years before the majority of the school shootings began in the late 1980s.

But the Anthony Barbaro school shooting was much different than the others due to Barbaro's background.

Unlike all of the other notorious school shooters mentioned above, Barbaro exhibited few if any of the warning signs of a potential mass murderer. If anything, Barbaro was very atypical in his profile: he got along with his fellow classmates and teachers, had no problems at home, and was a good student with a bright future.

Somehow Anthony Barbaro fell through the cracks.

An Honor Student

Anthony Barbaro was born in 1958 to a middle-class family in Olean, New York. Although in the state of New York, Olean is located in the western part of the state on the Pennsylvania state line far from New York City. The closest major city to Olean is Buffalo, but residents of the town like to see themselves far from big city life.

Olean has traditionally been a politically conservative town where guns and pickup trucks are more common than yoga studios and coffee shops. The town came to prominence in the late nineteenth century when it was part of the Pennsylvania oil boom. Immigrants from Europe and around the world flocked to the Olean to work in nearby oil fields, which helped the population of the town peak at over 20,000 in the middle of the twentieth century.

The Barbaros were descended from hard-working Italian immigrants who came to the area during the oil boom. By the time Anthony was born, the Barbaro family were well respected in the community, playing a prominent role in their local Catholic parish and volunteering in various civic groups. Anthony's father had a well-paying position as an executive at an engineering firm and his mother was a full-time mother and worked part-time at a local fast food restaurant. Anthony and his two younger siblings, a brother and sister, had everything they needed and there was no abuse of any type in the Barbaro home.

Everything was fine in Anthony Barbaro's home life.

Barbaro's school and social life also appear to have been stable. Anthony had a circle of friends whom he regularly spent time with, none of which ever stated that he made violent threats or ever talked about violence in general. He also worked part-time with his mother at the fast food restaurant and was said to be a good employee with no problems.

In terms of academics, Anthony Barbaro was at the top of his class. School seemed to be easy for the teenager, who was a senior at Olean High School during the 1974-1975 school year. Although he spent a fair amount of time studying, homework came easy to Anthony so he was able to dedicate his time to other pursuits.

When he wasn't studying, working at the fast food restaurant, or spending time with his friends or family, Anthony was taking part in extracurricular activities at his high school. He was on the bowling team for a short time, but was cut. Those who knew him at the time said that he didn't seem very upset about getting cut from the team and it is generally not considered to play a role in his later actions.

The extracurricular activity that Anthony Barbaro excelled in was shooting.

It was once common for many high schools in rural America to have rifle teams and still is in many western states. So it was common in the 1970s to see high school students carrying rifles around town on their way to competitions or to practice at ranges, which could be anything from an official indoor range to a field in the middle of nowhere.

Anthony was the star on his team, which he achieved by regular practice with his own 30-06 rifle.

Early in his senior year, Anthony learned that his grades, combined with his extracurricular activities earned him a scholarship to the prestigious New York University in New York City.

Most kids in his position would've been thrilled, but Anthony kept his feelings to himself. He told his parents that he was happy about the news, but that he didn't want to celebrate it. In fact, Anthony Barbaro was known to be quite reserved, almost brooding, when it came to his feelings.

Because of that, no one thought anything was amiss with the young scholar on the afternoon of December 30, 1974.

The Massacre

On December 30th, Anthony and his siblings were enjoying the time off from school for Christmas break, at least Anthony's brother and sister were. Anthony spent part of the morning watching television with his ten-year-old brother Chris and then around noon told him that he was going to practice shooting.

Chris didn't think his brother was going to practice on humans.

Since Anthony was a star shooter on his school's team, his parents let him take his rifle out regularly without permission. They reasoned that Anthony was a bright, responsible young man who knew the dangerous capabilities of a loaded gun.

They were right about their son, but for the wrong reasons.

After he retrieved his gun, he apparently took a meandering route to the high school because he did not arrive there until about 2:50 pm. No one knows what Anthony did in the time between he left the Barbaro home until he arrived at Olean High School, but it is probable that he took some time to consider what he was about to do. Unlike some other notorious school shooters, Anthony Barbaro didn't leave what can be considered a manifesto, so it is conjecture to consider how long he had been planning his assault.

With that said, the details of the massacre clearly show that

Anthony Barbaro had been thinking about and had been planning the assault on the high school for some time.

When Barbaro arrived at Olean High School just before three, he entered the school through an unlocked door. Since classes were out for break, most of the school was locked, but there was still a skeleton crew of janitors and maintenance workers there, which is why one of the doors was unlocked.

Once Barbaro gained entry into the school, he headed for the student council room on the third floor. It was there that he set off a smoke bomb in front of the room, which was probably intended to obscure the origins of his gunfire.

The smoke bomb had the unintended effect of setting off the fire alarm, which brought the workers on duty to the source but also covered Barbaro's gunfire as he shot his way into the student council room. Once inside the student council room, Barbaro was ready to go to work.

Earl Metcaff was the first janitor to respond to the disturbance on the third floor. According to his co-workers who were also working at the school at the time, he thought it was some kids pulling a prank.

It was no prank.

As Barbaro was setting up in the student council room to begin his massacre, he saw Metcaff approaching the room from a window that faced the hallway. Without hesitation, Barbaro used his well-honed shooting skills to dispatch the unsuspecting janitor with one shot.

Things were just getting started.

Barbaro then moved to a window facing the street and began indiscriminately shooting at pedestrians on the street below and then the first responders who showed up to help them.

The small town of Olean suddenly became a war zone.

The crazed teen shooter next shot and killed a twenty-five-year-old mother named Carmen Drayton, who happened to be driving by the school. He then spied meter reader Neal Pilon across the street and killed him with a single shot.

Barbaro then turned his wrath on the firefighters who were trying to rescue the wounded, injuring eight.

Besides the three lives he claimed, Barbaro wounded eleven others during the course of his shooting spree. The local police and sheriff's departments were unable to stop the assault, so the New York State Police and the national guard were called.

Three hours after the massacre began, state police officers shot tear gas cannisters into the room Barbaro was using as his gun turret. But the intelligent young man seemed to think of everything and was equipped with a gas mask.

Fortunately for the people of Olean, Barbaro's gas mask was defective.

The police found Barbaro unconscious in the student council room. He was quickly cuffed and whisked away to the county jail where he was charged with murder.

Unanswered Questions

Although Barbaro was a juvenile at the time of the massacre, he was charged as an adult due to the severity of the crimes and because he was nearly eighteen. Barbaro was charged with a total of fourteen felonies, which included: three counts of second-degree murder, six counts of first-degree assault, and five counts of first-degree reckless endangerment. Although the murders were clearly planned, New York state statues reserve the charge of first-degree murder for only a select few types of murders, such as the murder of a police officer.

Still, Anthony Barbaro was looking at spending the rest of his life in prison.

Barbaro was remanded to the adult section of the Cattaraugus County Jail, but was placed in an isolated cell block for his own protection. He was denied bail, which came as no surprise because bail is usually not given in cases that involve multiple murders.

Barbaro pleaded not guilty by reason of insanity. If a jury or a judge had found in Barbaro's favor, it would have probably meant a lifetime in a secured mental hospital for the once promising student.

Instead of going away to college in the fall of 1975, Anthony Barbaro sat in a cell in the Cattaraugus County Jail awaiting his fate. He had a lot of time to think about his actions and spent his time like many jail inmates do, writing letters to friends, family, and the occasional criminal groupie. Like many other high-profile criminals who came before and after him, Barbaro developed a relationship with a young woman through letter writing. Although his pen pal never visited him, they seem to have developed a deep bond as evidenced by some of the letters they exchanged, especially the last letter Barbaro sent her.

As Barbaro's case slowly worked its way through the system, everyone in western New York repeatedly asked the same question: why?

A clear answer never came. On November 1, 1975, Anthony Barbaro was found hanging in his cell. Efforts to revive him were unsuccessful. A thorough search of his cell turned up three suicide notes that were similar in their overall context, but differed in details. One was addressed to his family, one to the young woman he was writing, and another "to whom it may concern."

The notes were articulate and introspective, which only created more mystery surrounding Barbaro's murderous motives. The note addressed "to whom it may concern" partially reads:

"I guess I just wanted to kill the person I hate most -- myself, I just didn't have the courage. I wanted to die, but I couldn't do it, so I had to get someone to do it for me. It didn't work out."

It continued:

"People are not afraid to die; it's just how they die. I don't fear death, but rather the pain. But no more. I regret the foods I'll never taste, the music I'll never hear, the sites I'll never see, the accomplishments I'll never accomplish, in other words, I regret my life. Some will always ask, 'Why?' I don't know — no one will. What has been, can't be changed. I'm sorry. It ends like it began; in the middle of the night, someone might think it selfish or cowardly to take one's own life. Maybe so, but it's the only free choice I have. The way I figure, I lose either way. If I'm found not guilty, I won't survive the pain I've caused — my guilt. If I'm convicted, I won't survive the mental and physical punishment of my life in prison."

Perhaps the letters demonstrate just how tragic this case was. In some ways, Anthony Barbaro possessed a wisdom that few adults have, but unfortunately, for some reason, he couldn't reconcile whatever drove him to violence with his precocious mind. Barbaro could have done much with his life and would've no doubt been a benefit to society.

Instead, Anthony Barbaro will always be remembered as a mass murderer and a school shooter.

CHAPTER 6:
The Murder of Harold Sasko

This volume of true crime cases includes many heinous crimes committed by young offenders. The reasons vary, but the results of the crime have all left people shaking their heads and wondering why young people would commit such horrific acts. Some cases, such as Anthony Barbaro's shooting spree, defy explanation and have no true motives, but maybe worse are the teen "thrill kills."

Unfortunately, the annals of criminal history are full of many thrill kills. Whether it is a sadistic military commander, a serial killer, or a young person, all thrill killers are driven by an unnatural desire to see other humans in pain and to watch them die.

Most cases of thrill kills, especially among serial killers, are stranger on stranger crimes. The killer usually picks his victim, or victims, out of convenience, although other factors also play a role.

But sometimes those closest to you are thrill killers, looking at you everyday the way a cat does a mouse, waiting for the right time to pounce and sadistically play with you before ending your life.

This is exactly what happened to fifty-two-year-old Kansas entrepreneur Harold Sasko when he offered to share his home with a troubled young woman. When Sasko was found stabbed to death in his Lawrence, Kansas home in January 2014, suspicion immediately fell on his nineteen-year-old roommate, employee, and possible lover, Sarah Gonzalez McLinn.

When the local authorities finally revealed the details behind Sasko's murder, the public was surprised to learn of a bizarre plot that included plenty of drugs, booze, and a desire to kill for no other reason than to see how it felt.

Some say Sako was killed for doing a good deed while others believed that he was the victim of a May-September romance gone wrong.

Whatever the circumstances, it was clear that Gonzalez McLinn killed Sasko for her own satisfaction.

An Unlikely Pair

Harold Sasko and Sarah Gonzalez McLinn came from two completely different worlds. That was the partial result of them being from two generations. Sasko, a late Baby Boomer, was thirty-three years Gonzalez McLinn's senior and officially two generations ahead of the young Millennial. It would not be an exaggeration to say that Sasko grew up in quite a different country than what Gonzalez McLinn knew as a child.

A native Kansan, Sasko was the tenth of twelve children in what can be described as a typical post-war, Midwestern family. The Saskos were church going people who instilled those values in their children along with a strong work ethic and the value of earning and saving money.

The values especially resonated with young Harold.

After graduating high school, Harold worked a number of different jobs before realizing that he had a knack for numbers and business. He operated a number of successful businesses and eventually got married. Sasko and his wife had a daughter, but like many marriages today, they eventually drifted apart and divorced.

But Sasko's ambition never diminished.

By the 1990s, Sasko became involved in the fairly new, Texas-based restaurant chain Cici's Pizza. Eventually, Sasko bought two Cici's franchises in Topeka, Kansas and one in his hometown of Lawrence.

For the most part, Sasko lived a quiet, suburban lifestyle in a middle-class neighborhood of Lawrence. He got along well with his neighbors and most who knew him described him as a "good guy."

Sasko's friends and family said that he often went out of his way to help people, even those he didn't know very well. They said that he particularly had a soft spot for his employees, many of whom were young with various problems. Sasko was willing to take a chance and hire anyone who he thought would work hard, including people who were recently released from jail and/or a treatment center.

With his daughter living with his ex-wife fulltime, Sasko seemed to find surrogate children among his many employees. He allowed one of his employees to use his car for a vacation and helped another one get a loan so that he could buy a car.

Harold Sasko's generosity toward his employees seemed to know no bounds.

Then in 2013, he told the woman he was dating that he was allowing an eighteen-year-old female employee to move into his home. He explained that the employee had a difficult home life and that she was having a tough time finding a place to stay. The girlfriend didn't like the fact that such a young woman would be living in the same house with Sasko, but he was intent on helping the employee.

The employee was Sarah Gonzalez McLinn.

About the only thing that Gonzalez McLinn had in common with Sasko was that they were both born in the same state. Born nearly two generations after Sasko, Gonzalez McLinn grew up in a very different Kansas. Born in the mid-1990s, Gonzalez McLinn barely knew her father and was raised exclusively by her mother and her mother's family.

The McLinns learned at an early point that Sarah was going to have problems.

In her quest to connect with her Hispanic father, Sarah began running with kids of various Hispanic backgrounds on the streets of Topeka. The image she had of her father was for the most part negative – according to the McLinn family, Gonzalez had rightfully earned that reputation – but it was also "cool" to a teenager who wanted to be rebellious. Because of that, Sarah often sought out the criminal elements in the Hispanic community of Topeka. Although the McLinns tried to pull her away from the negative influences, she kept going back to find her missing father figure.

Sarah developed a drug habit in her early teens and often associated with known gang members.

By the age of eighteen, Sarah Gonzalez McLinn's life was a mess.

As the young woman's life seemed to spiral out of control, she found employment at a Cici's Pizza owned by Harold Sasko. According to his friends, Harold soon learned about Sarah's difficult childhood and the fact that she was still having problems finding a place to live.

To Harold's friends and family, they believe he saw Sarah as a "project."

"To me, I think he saw it as a project to fix, to help make better," said Harold's brother, Glenn about Gonzalez McLinn.

Gonzalez McLinn had been living at Harold's for just a few short months by January 14, 2014. By all accounts, the two got along fine and the living arrangement seemed to be going well. Some of

Harold's employees even thought that the situation was going so well that it was more than platonic.

Harold and Sarah usually went to work together and on the days when Harold didn't work, or when he was at one of his other stores, he usually made it back to drive Sarah home. To this day it is unknown if the pair developed a romantic relationship, but it would not be unlikely considering how much time they spent together.

Whether they were romantically involved or not, it was clear to all who knew them that they got along quite well, which is partially what made the events of January 14th so shocking.

The Murder

The exact circumstances that led to the tragic events on January 14th remain murky, but based on Gonzalez McLinn's later confession and the forensic evidence, a reasonable outline can be drawn. Both Sarah and Harold had the evening off and decided to spend it at the house drinking some beers. Harold apparently thought it was just going to be a quiet night in, but Sarah had other ideas.

At some point during the evening, Gonzalez McLinn put her devious plan into action when Harold wasn't looking. She crushed several Ambien sleeping pills into a powder and put it into Harold's beer. The bitter taste of the beer apparently masked the taste of the powdered pills because Sasko readily drank the concoction.

It didn't take long for him to pass out.

As Harold was lying on the floor of his house unconscious, Sarah bound his arms and legs with zip ties and gagged his mouth. The actions were entirely superfluous, though, since Sasko had enough alcohol and Ambien in his system to incapacitate him for several hours.

Gonzalez McLinn then proceeded to the next phase of her plan.

Making sure to hit the right spot, Sarah aimed a knife straight for Harold's neck, severing arteries and veins in the process. She stabbed him a few more times for good measure, but the defenseless pizzeria entrepreneur would've died from the first stab.

Apparently, Gonzalez McLinn never considered what she'd do after she killed Sasko. She was too small to move Sasko's body and Sarah was determined to not involve anyone else.

She had few options at this point.

Some criminals would attempt to burn the house in order to cover up forensic evidence, but Gonzalez McLinn was not much of a criminal, nor very bright.

She decided to go on the run.

It is obvious that Gonzalez McLinn had no real plan to live on the lam as evidenced by nearly every decision she made after killing Sasko. After killing Harold, Sarah simply left the house, and all of the physical evidence, as is and fled in Sasko's 2008 Nissan Altima with his dog.

From Lawrence, Sarah drove hundreds of miles south to Bishop, Texas near the U.S.-Mexican border, apparently in an attempt to evade justice by hiding out in Mexico. Something made Sarah change her mind, though, and she instead drove hundreds more miles to Florida. While in Florida, she slept in Sasko's car and camped out illegally in and around the Everglades.

Meanwhile, back in Kansas, Gonzalez McLinn's family reported her missing on January 17th . When she never showed up for a family dinner on the 14th, which of course was the night she murdered Sasko, her family immediately thought nothing of it. They reasoned that, lately Sarah had become more responsible and probably decided to pick up an extra shift at work. She would call them soon to let them know what happened.

But when Sarah never called, her family began to worry.

The McLinns worried that Sarah had drifted back into her old crowd and was using drugs again, or worse, some of her old associates had done something to her. They called the police who went to Sasko's home to search for the missing young adult, but instead found the mutilated body of a middle-aged man.

A warrant was immediately issued for Sarah Gonzalez McLinn's arrest.

Not long after the warrant was issued in Kansas, local police arrested Gonzalez McLinn in Florida for camping in a park after hours. A search of her/Sasko's car turned up a small amount of marijuana and prescription pills that were not in her name.

The police also found an axe and two knives that are believed to have been used in Sasko's murder.

It didn't take long for Gonzalez McLinn's warrant to show up on the Florida police computers, so she was held without bond awaiting police from Douglass County, Kansas to fly down to Florida. Douglass County detectives were surprised to learn that not only was Gonzalez McLinn not going to fight extradition to Kansas, but that she was also willing to give a complete confession to Sasko's murder.

In the long and rambling confession, Sarah told the detectives that she had been having violent thoughts and fantasies for some time and that she "wanted to know what it felt like" to kill someone.

The detectives were shocked to learn that the young, seemingly innocent looking girl in front of them took a human life just for the thrill.

An Insanity Defense

When Gonzalez McLinn was finally brought back to Kansas and given court-appointed lawyers, it was time for them to create a legal defense. But there was a mountain of evidence stacked against their client. Besides her lengthy confession, there were several other pieces of circumstantial and physical evidence that squarely pointed toward Gonzalez McLinn's guilt.

Sarah's flight after the killing showed signs of premeditation, or at least the recognition that she had done something wrong, which would work against any type of insanity defense. DNA taken from the weapons recovered from Sasko's car matched the murdered entrepreneur and the toxicology report showed that he had ingested six Ambien tablets, further proof of premeditation. The final piece of evidence that showed Gonzalez McLinn premeditated her roommate's murder, was a series of Google searches someone in the home made using phrases such as "neck vulnerable spots."

After carefully reviewing all of the evidence, Gonzalez McLinn's attorneys knew that they would have a nearly impossible time getting a jury to convict their client of anything less than first-degree murder. In many such murder cases, lawyers often see convictions for lesser offenses, such as second-degree murder or manslaughter, as a victory when their clients are facing first-degree murder charges and a possible sentence of life without the possibility of parole, or even the death penalty.

Sarah's lawyers knew they had to take a different path, so they decided to try an insanity defense.

Insanity defenses are rarely successful in the United States and even when they are, the defendant is usually placed in a secured mental hospital for an indeterminate period, often the rest of his or her life.

Still, Gonzalez McLinn's lawyers argued it was better than the alternative of life in prison with no parole.

The defense called experts to the stand who testified that Sarah suffered from dissociative disorder, which is when the person afflicted believes he or she has multiple, distinct personalities. The experts said that a personality named "Alyssa" was Sarah's murderous alter-ego and that it was essentially uncontrollable.

The jury didn't buy the insanity defense.

On March 20, 2015, Sarah Gonzalez McLinn was found guilty of first-degree murder. Later that year she was sentenced to what is known as the "hard fifty" in the state of Kansas, or a fifty year minimum behind bars.

Sarah will have plenty of time to reflect on what she did and if she really does suffer from dissociative disorder, then she will be able to receive treatment in prison. Due to her young age, there is a possibility that Sarah will be released from prison one day, but she will be an elderly woman no longer able to pose the threat of committing another thrill kill.

Or will she? Only time can tell.

CHAPTER 7:
The Murder of the Doss Family

As evidenced by several of the chapters in this volume, youth violence is a scourge that doesn't appear to be going away anytime soon. Youth violence has been recorded throughout history, but the especially heinous cases, are for the most part, a modern phenomenon and relegated to the last four decades. Although the crime rate in the United States dropped in the early 1980s, youth crime increased.

Gang violence has plagued America's inner cities, but a new breed of seemingly conscienceless youth criminals emerged from the suburbs and rural areas beginning in the 1970s. Sociologists argue that this group of youth criminals are often spurred by a lack of direction, which leads to thrill-seeking in the forms of illicit drug use and other criminal activity.

But that doesn't explain the sheer brutality of many of these crimes.

Many of these youth murders are extremely sadistic when compared to other murder cases and as the case of Anthony Barbaro demonstrates, sometimes there is no apparent motive.

The next case, like Barbaro's, involves a juvenile killer who took innocent people's lives for no known reason. After that fact, though, this case diverges significantly.

On May 11, 2011, the bodies of thirty-four-year-old Amanda Prewett Doss and her two children, eleven-year-old Guinevere Doss and eight-year-old Texas Johnson were discovered in their burned up Redwater, Texas home. The subsequent investigation revealed that the family had been murdered and the fire was set to cover the crimes.

The news sent the Texarkana, Texas and Arkansas area into a panic.

The initial investigation eventually went cold, but when it was eventually solved residents of the area were shocked to learn that the perpetrator was a juvenile girl. It set many people's notions about crime upside down, but reaffirmed the ideas of those who knew about the ever-increasing problem of youth violence in the United States.

A Bizarre Case

As soon as the investigation into the murders of the Doss family began, it was immediately shrouded in mystery. The case began when Amanda Doss' parents received a frantic phone call on the night of May 11 from Guinevere, who was screaming into the phone for her grandparents to come help. The disturbed grandparents phoned 911 and then raced over to their daughter's home only to find it engulfed in flames.

First responders arrived shortly after Amanda's family, but were unable to rescue anyone from the inferno.

The investigators were interested to know about the phone call that Guinevere made to her grandparents, but unfortunately she gave no details about her plight. With the phone call being an apparent dead end, the investigators turned to the burned home and the bodies recovered from it for answers.

An autopsy revealed that Amanda and her two children had been stabbed to death. It remained unknown if sexual assault had occurred, but fire investigators were able to prove that the fire was deliberate and no doubt set to eliminate any physical evidence left at the scene.

The homicide investigators immediately thought they were dealing with a sophisticated, possibly career criminal. To them, it seemed to have all the hallmarks of a pro: there were no witnesses left and the arson was clearly done to destroy any physical evidence. Of course, anyone could do those things, but their experience told them that the chances were that the murders were done by someone well-acquainted with the criminal underworld.

The fathers of Amanda's children were questioned first along with all of the other men in her life, but their alibis were all rock solid. The detectives then widened their net to include known sex offenders in the area, as well as other career criminals who had burglary, kidnapping, and/or arson on their rap sheets.

Although a few interesting leads turned up, no viable suspects emerged.

Eventually, in what was perhaps somewhat of a desperate move, a $145,000 reward was offered that would lead to the arrests of the Doss family's killer or killers.

As the months went by, leads about the case began to evaporate until there were none.

The Doss Family

As no viable leads concerning the identity of the Doss family's killer, or killers, never panned out, residents of Redwater repeatedly asked, who would want to kill Amanda and her children?

No one could come up with an answer.

Amanda was an attractive single mother who, although garnered significant attention from potential suitors, was more interested in the welfare of her children. She worked full-time but like with many single mothers, found it difficult to juggle work and her children. Her parents weren't always available to watch her children and she got little help from her children's fathers.

Luckily Rachael Pittman lived nearby.

Rachael Pittman was a sixteen-year-old girl who lived a few miles away from the Doss family in 2011. Like most kids her age,

Rachael wanted to have her own money and the independence that goes with it, so she started babysitting in her early teens. Amanda Doss was introduced to Rachael through a mutual acquaintance as a potential babysitter who would work at a reduced fee.

Amanda was pleased with Rachael's work, as she appeared to get along well with her children and was reliable.

But Rachael lived in her own world. It was a world that she kept most people, including her own family, out of and it was indeed a dark world. She had few friends and unlike many kids without friends her age, she seemed to not want any friends. In the days immediately after the murders of the Doss family, Rachael Pittman's mother said she didn't seem very disturbed by the events but rationalized that everyone grieves differently.

Rachael's behavior seemed to get stranger, until one day about three months after the Doss murders, she gave her mom some disturbing news – she was the person who killed Amanda and her family. At first, Rachael's mom didn't believe what she had just heard and told her to quit joking. She had become accustomed to Rachael's sometimes strange behavior and macabre sense of humor, but deep down she knew that this was different.

After Rachael insisted that she was telling the truth, her mother immediately reported the confession to the police.

Rachael Pittman was arrested on three counts of capital murder as a juvenile.

Arrest and Trial

Although a capital murder charge in the state of Texas means that the defendant could face the death penalty, Rachael was not eligible as a juvenile and even if certified as an adult, she could still not be executed due to federal law.

Still, many of the residents of metro Texarkana wanted to see Rachael on death row.

Texas is a "law and order" state where most of the residents are more than willing to "throw the book" at an offender, no matter the person's gender or age.

But it was precisely Rachael Pittman's gender and age that had so many people scratching their heads. Robbery was not apparently the motive and since Rachael was said to have gotten along so well with Amanda's children, revenge doesn't appear to have been a factor.

And as much as the local and state media were trying to get a story, the judge placed a gag order on the case, so Rachel's statement to the police was never released to the public.

Despite the death penalty being off the table due to Pittman's age when she committed the crimes, the prosecutor still pushed to charge her as an adult, which meant that she faced the possibility of spending the rest of her life in a tough Texas prison.

On February 9, 2012, the judge agreed with the prosecutor and ruled that Rachael Pittman would be tried as an adult.

Besides Rachael's confession to her mother, there was little evidence that pointed toward Pittman committing the triple murder. Because of this, she was initially confident of her chances in court and planned to take the case to trial. But as both sides prepared for a potentially long trial, the prosecutors presented Rachel with crime scene photos of her victims. According to her lawyers, the photos deeply troubled their young client who then decided to change her plea to guilty and throw herself at the mercy of the court.

In January 2013, Rachael Pittman was given two life sentences for first-degree murder. She will be eligible for parole in thirty years when she is in her mid-forties.

Most of the people involved with the case and the majority of the people of Redwater were for the most part pleased with the resolution of the case. They believed justice had been served and now the community could move forward.

But not everyone shared those sentiments.

Conspiracy Theories

Almost as soon as Pittman was taken into the custody of the Texas Department of Corrections, many people in the Texarkana area began asking questions that never came up at trial. Many thought that there was much more to the case than the public was being told, which led to many different conspiracy theories being propagated.

The judge's gag ruling did little to quell many of the questions and only seemed to add to the paranoia. People argued that they could understand why the judge thought it was prudent to impose a gag order during the trial, but they didn't understand why the ruling was kept in place even after Pittman was sent to prison.

Because of the gag ruling, it will remain unknown if Pittman related a motive for the triple murder to the police.

The average person around Texarkana familiar with the case, though, was more interested in Rachael Pittman's ability to kill three people than her motive. Many people thought it is nearly impossible for a sixteen-year-old, especially a girl, to kill three people and get away with it for months.

Rumors began to swirl around Texarkana that Pittman was merely helping some mysterious woman. The rumor/conspiracy theory held that the mysterious woman who was really the brains behind the murders became a suspect in the investigation at one point and she even failed a polygraph test. The local police, though, were unable to make a case against the woman so they had to let her go. The authorities then bowed to local pressure to close the case, so they arrested Pittman, who was involved in the murders according to the theory, and then quickly closed the case.

There is no evidence to support the conspiracy theory, but until the documents pertaining to the case are released to the public, conspiracy theories will no doubt continue to flourish.

CHAPTER 8:

The Teen Hatchet Killers, Antonio Barbeau and Nathan Paape

All of the many youth crimes profiled in this volume are truly terrible and shocking. The obvious question asked in the course of most of these cases is, how could a seemingly innocent kid be so violent and emotionally damaged? Did something happen to make them that way or were they just born "bad"?

These are, of course, questions that have been asked repeatedly and in most cases will probably never be answered. Sometimes it is important to look at the victim.

With the exception of Jeffrey Franklin, the other examples of youth violence profiled in this volume were non-familial assaults and murders. Excuses and self-defense arguments can always be made, whether legitimate or not, when someone kills a stranger or non-family member.

Justification gets infinitely more difficult when family members are involved and people in general see such crimes as inherently worse. For example, Lyle and Erik Menendez argued that they killed their father in retaliation for years of physical, sexual, and emotional abuse, which many people were willing to consider; but the murder of their mother was a bridge too far for most.

Probably even worse than patricide or matricide would be the killing of a grandparent.

Grandparents are traditionally the family members who give one the most unconditional love, even more than parents. Most grandparents who are involved in the lives of their grandchildren offer an extra shoulder to cry on and usually spoil their grandkids with money, food, and other items.

Why would anyone want to kill a grandparent like that?

On September 17, 2012, the small town of Sheboygan Falls, Wisconsin was riveted when it was learned that one of its elderly residents was brutally beaten to death in her own home. Most thought that a drug addict drifter would be the culprit, but were perplexed to learn that the killers were the woman's thirteen-year-old grandson and his friend.

Murders rarely happened in Sheboygan Falls and they were never perpetrated by thirteen-year-old boys on their grandmothers.

Quiet Sheboygan Falls

Located less than an hour's drive north of Milwaukee off Interstate 43, Sheboygan Falls, Wisconsin is a small town that eventually became a bedroom community exurb of Milwaukee.

For the most part, crime is an extremely rare phenomenon in Sheboygan Falls and murder is almost unheard of – before 2012, the last murder in the town happened in 1996.

It is truly the type of town that people like because it is somewhat far removed from the problems of big city Milwaukee, but still close enough to drive to for work, shopping, or other things. By 2012, Sheboygan Falls' residents are a mix of two groups. Many are younger families who have moved there to escape the crime, congestion, and higher taxes of Milwaukee. Many of these people commute back and forth from Milwaukee and see the town more as a place to sleep at night than a community that they are a part of. The other group consists of the residents whose families have lived in the town for generations. These people are generally more invested in the town and take the extra step to know their neighbors and to take part in civic activities and events.

Barbara Olson was in the latter category.

Olson had called Sheboygan Falls her home for her entire life. The seventy-eight-year-old great grandmother had raised a family in the quiet town that she loved so much. When many of her retried and elderly friends began moving to Florida, Texas, and Arizona to beat the long Wisconsin winters, Olson remained steadfast in her love of the area. She was the typical upper Midwesterner who may complain about the heavy snow and sub-zero temperatures in the middle of the winter, but she actually would never had traded it in for life in Florida.

Barbara Olson had everything she needed in Sheboygan Falls: her friends, children, and grandchildren, including Antonio Barbeau.

In September 2012, Antonio Barbeau and Nathan Paape had just started the eighth grade. Simply put, there was nothing extraordinary about either of the two boys. They didn't participate in any extracurricular activities at their junior high school and neither did very well in their course work.

Neither boy was ever accused of being very bright.

Antonio's family would later claim that a serious car accident he was in at the age of ten left him mentally disabled. Nathan also showed signs of being developmentally slow.

Although it looked like neither of the two boys would ever go on to do great things, they never showed signs of problematic behavior, either. Besides some minor infractions, neither of the two ever were in serious trouble at school and most adults who knew them said they were for the most part respectful.

The boys showed particular respect and affection toward Barbara Olson. Barbara was Antonio's maternal grandmother and in true grandmotherly nature, she often doted on Antonio, whom she saw as an underdog. Antonio and Nathan would spend hours on end at Barbara's, watching television, playing in the backyard, and trading sports cards. Barbara was always happy to have her grandkids stop by for visits, but Antonio began to change during the summer of 2012 to the point where she became leery of him.

Antonio and Nathan were living in their own world at that point.

The two boys spent their free time almost exclusively together – they really didn't have other friends or girlfriends. For the most part, their parents were involved in their lives, but gave them a certain amount of freedom.

They rarely asked the boys what they were doing and never pried.

The events of September 17th made them wish they had.

A Ridiculous Plot

The authorities later learned that Barbeau's and Paape's attack was premeditated and had been planned for some time. With that said, it is important to remember that the two perpetrators were thirteen-year-old boys who were not exactly at the top of their class.

Their complete lack of understanding of consequences was manifested when they decided to kill Barbara Olson for monetary gain.

In the months before the murder, the two boys learned that they liked marijuana. Despite living in a small town and being quite young, they had no problem getting access to marijuana, but had problems raising funds. They were both too young to work legally at stores or restaurants and neither had the gumption to make money mowing lawns and/or shoveling driveways and sidewalks.

Antonio suggested robbing his grandmother.

The two boys were under the assumption that the retired grandmother who lived on a fixed income was wealthy. They floated different ideas to get Olson's money, such as burglary, but came to the conclusion that murder would be the best option for them to get some weed.

When school got out on the afternoon of September 17th, Barbeau went over to Paape's house as he often did. But on this day, instead of hanging out, the two boys were doing their final preparations for murder. Antonio pulled out a hatchet and showed Nathan, who was impressed with the weapon. For his part, Nathan grabbed a hammer from the garage.

The two boys were ready to kill a grandma for some weed money.

About an hour after meeting up at Paape's house, Nathan's mother gave the two boys a ride to Barbara Olson's. After saying goodbye to Nathan's mom, the two boys told her that they would find their own way back home later.

Barbeau and Paape then went to the side of the garage that was connected to the house to put their nefarious plan into action. Once in the garage, they planned to stealthily enter the house and surprise Barbara, but she heard sounds in the garage and opened the door to greet them.

The details of what happened next are a bit murky, because although both boys confessed to the crime, they pointed the finger at each other in court, so it is difficult to say which one attacked first. The autopsy revealed that Barbara was struck at least twenty-seven times with the axe and hammer. After the duo hit the defenseless old woman several times, she collapsed in the doorway.

The two criminal masterminds planned to drag the small woman's body to her car, where they planned to put her in the trunk and then dispose of her in a rural area. It seemed so easy as they both had seen it done so many times on television.

But the two thirteen-year-old dimwits quickly learned that t.v. is not reality.

After having problems trying to move Barbara's body to the car, they decided to give up the endeavor and leave her in the garage for someone to find, probably one of Antonio's relatives. The pair then pillaged the house for anything of value and came up with $150 in cash and some jewelry.

Score!

The two boys then put the final phase of their plan into action, whereby they thought they would place the blame for the murder on someone else. They drove Barbara's car to a local bowling alley known to be frequented by some of the local toughs and left the keys in the ignition with the jewelry they had stolen on the front seat.

Feeling that all of a sudden life was good, the boys then bought a bag of pot and a large pepperoni pizza.

The Discovery

As ridiculous as Barbeau's and Paape's murder plot was, it was two days before any suspicion was cast their way. In the two days after killing Barbara Olson, Barbeau and Paape spent their time smoking pot and watching television.

They hadn't a care in the world.

On September 19th, one of Barbara's daughters came by the house for a routine visit. She didn't think anything was wrong with her mother, but the children liked to take turns checking up on her. As soon as she entered the garage, she was horrified to find her mother dead in a pool of blood.

The police were immediately called and within hours, Barbara's car was located in the bowling alley parking lot. The police recognized that the car's placement and the jewelry on the front seat was to throw them off and to possibly entice someone to steal the car, the jewelry, or both.

They also recognized that everything looked like the work of an amateur.

Once the police determined that there was no forced entry into Barbara's house and that it actually looked like she opened the door for her killer, they began to focus on those closest to the pensioner.

Barbeau's and Paape's names came up as possibly the last two people to see her alive; but no one could see how two thirteen-year-olds could do such a thing, especially since Antonio was Barbara's grandson.

Still, police officers generally have good intuition, which was sending them more and more in the boys' direction.

A search of Antonio's locker at school turned up bloody clothing, which led to a search warrant to search both of their homes. A search of the Paape home turned up more bloody clothing.

Antonio Barbeau and Nathan Paape were charged with the first-degree murder of Barbara Olson as adults.

But things were just getting started.

Pointing the Finger

Although Barbeau and Paape were only thirteen when they killed Barbara, the county prosecutors thought that the crime was heinous enough to get the two charged as adults. After a hearing to decide the matter, a judge agreed and certified the duo as adults.

If convicted, the boys faced the prospect of spending the rest of their lives in a maximum security prison for adult men.

Needless to say, the two boys were frightened of the prospect and immediately set about to defend themselves in court. But the reality was that they had little defense. Although they pointed the finger at each other almost immediately, they both gave statements implicating themselves in the plot and both placed themselves at the crime scene. Still, their attorneys were bound to put up credible defenses.

The boys' attorneys succeeded in their first battle – severing the two cases into separate trials. By doing that, they could more logically point the finger at one another. It would only take one juror to believe the story, thereby getting a mistrial.

Despite severing the cases, both boys' lawyers put up similar defenses – "he made me do it!"

Before going to trial, though, Barbeau's lawyers decided to play one final card that could keep their client from spending the remainder of his life in prison. They had Antonio plead not guilty by reason of mental disease or defect, arguing that the injuries he sustained in the car accident several years prior left him unable to process right and wrong like a normal person.

As Barbeau's lawyers were preparing his defense, the influence of the boy's family, combined with possibly a guilty conscience began to take hold. The extended Olson family didn't want to see a lengthy trial, so some began urging Barbeau's parents to convince him to take a plea bargain.

The prosecutor didn't offer Barbeau a plea bargain, but the teenager still changed his original not guilty plea to no contest in June 2013. He essentially threw himself at the court. On August 12, 2013, Antonio Barbeau was given the very adult sentence of life in prison with the possibility of parole after thirty-six years.

Around the time that Antonio pled no contest, Nathan went on trial. Paape made the rare move in a criminal trial of testifying in his own defense. His lawyers believed that doing so would help humanize their client and that it would be difficult for a jury to convict a fourteen-year-old boy of murder.

Paape's testimony was unconvincing.

In testimony that many thought looked well-rehearsed, Paape stated that he only hit Olson a couple of times and only did so because he was scared of Barbeau. Although the prosecutor treated Paape with kid gloves as he did the cross-examination, he did get the teen to admit that they took turns hitting Olson with the different weapons.

The jury didn't find Paape particularly convincing, convicting him of first-degree murder. The presiding judge later handed down a sentence of life in prison with the possibility of parole after thirty-one years.

"In my 24 years on the bench, I've not seen anything of this nature. Not even close," Circuit Court Judge Timothy Van Akkeren said in issuing his sentence. "It gives me great sadness to see someone of your age going into the system."

Despite the long sentences, since both were thirteen when they entered the system, they will probably be released one day. Will quiet Sheboygan Falls be ready for them?

CHAPTER 9:
Cody Alan Legebokoff – the Canadian Country Boy Killer

A cursory examination of modern serial killers reveals that they come in all shapes and sizes. Thanks to the modern media, though, there are many misconceptions common throughout society pertaining to serial killers. There seem to be two common serial killer archetypes portrayed in fictional movies, television shows, and books. The first is a middle-aged white male who is not very bright and an unemployed drifter.

The second archetype is also usually a middle-aged white male, but in contrast he is often depicted as highly intelligent, a genius even. The Hannibal Lecter character is perhaps most emblematic of this archetype, but one does not have to look long to find other serial killers portrayed as geniuses across a variety of media.

Although both of these archetypes have elements of reality, they are far from the truth.

The Radford University serial killer database, which is considered the definitive source of serial killer demographic information, has thrown a wrench into many misconceptions about serial killers. For instance, whites only make up over 50% of all serial killers in the United States, while blacks are close to 40%. It is true that women are far underrepresented in serial killing, with only 10% of all known serial killers being women and most serial killers are in their thirties or older, affirming the middle age stereotype.

There is a great range in IQ levels among serial killers, but the average comes out to about average IQ. Contrary to the unemployed drifter stereotype, most serial killers work – although not always steady jobs – and many have families and social networks.

Part of the reason why it is difficult to pigeonhole serial killers is because they are so diverse in their motives.

Most people commonly think of serial killers being driven by lust, such as Ted Bundy and Jeffrey Dahmer, and although that is a common motive, it is only one among many. Many serial killers care little about the act and are instead driven by financial rewards. Black widows, which are usually women, and hitmen, such as Richard Kuklinski, kill repeatedly for the comfort of financial rewards. Still, other serial killers operate under an idea that they are in the middle of a political war, such as Joseph Paul Franklin, which to them justifies all murders they commit.

Finally, there are serial killers who are driven by a combination of motives. These are the most difficult for the authorities to track because they often change their method of operation.

These are the serial killers who defy categorization.

In many ways, Corey Legebokoff also defied categorization and truly never fit any stereotype of what most would consider what a serial killer looks or acts like. Legebokoff has been described by many as an "all-Canadian boy." Coming from a decent family, Legebokoff was the quintessential western Canadian, who played hockey and enjoyed country music. He had a large network of friends, was charming and good-looking, and never displayed any violence around those who knew him.

It turns out that he was also one of Canada's youngest serial killers.

In his somewhat brief run as a serial killer, Legebokoff not only fooled everyone who knew him by being a good friend, family member, and employee on the one hand, while killing on the other; but he also displayed a startling amount of criminal sophistication for a young man with no criminal background. He learned the vocation of serial killing quickly and was able to adapt his method of operation to avoid detection.

If it weren't for a chance encounter with law enforcement on a lonely road, Corey Legebokoff might still be killing in the Great White North.

Just Another Canadian?

Corey Legebokoff was born in 1990 to a middle-class family in northern British Columbia. When most people think of British

Columbia, the cosmopolitan Vancouver comes to mind, but that was not the world where Legebokoff was raised.

Northern British Columbia, like Alberta, Saskatchewan, and Manitoba are very different than Vancouver or Toronto. In many ways, those areas are more like the western or even southern United States than they are the rest of Canada. The people of the western provinces, outside of Vancouver, tend to be much more conservative politically and live similar lifestyles to their American counterparts. Farming and ranching are a major part of the region's economy and the people have developed a hardy, self-sufficient attitude not seen in the rest of the country. Guns and pickup trucks are fairly common and country music is the most popular form of music.

Truly, many Canadians view the western provinces as their version of the American south.

Legebokoff appeared perfectly happy and well-adjusted in this environment as a child. He learned how to hunt and fish as a child and excelled in the truly Canadian sport of hockey. Corey also discovered that he had an aptitude for mechanical work at a young age and loved to tinker with boat and lawnmower motors. He eventually turned that love into a career as a mechanic.

Not long after Legebokoff graduated high school, he did what many young men do and left his home to see the world. For Legebokoff, that meant moving to Lethbridge, Alberta where he lived for a short time. But eventually he became homesick and moved back to northern British Columbia to build a life.

And a career as a budding serial killer.

Legebokoff ended up settling in Prince George, British Columbia, which at 75,000 people is the largest city in the northern part of the province. It is also one of the fastest growing cities in Canada, so Legebokoff had no problem finding work and a place to live. He quickly found work as a mechanic at a local Ford dealership and he used his extensive social connections from high school to find an apartment. His roommates were three young women who all claimed they felt safe around Legebokoff.

In late 2008 and early 2009, Corey Legebokoff looked far from being a future serial killer. His laid back, country boy persona made him a hit with the ladies and his life seemed to be going in the right direction. He was doing better financially than most people his age and had no problems to speak of.

But Corey Legebokoff had a dark side.

Many of Corey's friends knew that he liked to party heavily sometimes. He had quite a tolerance for alcohol and was known to do cocaine from time to time, but most of his friends never thought it was a problem – Corey never let his partying get out of hand.

Or so they thought.

By early 2009, Legebokoff's chemical use had gone from occasional all night partying to daily cocaine use. It was also around that time that he began frequenting prostitutes in Prince George, both for sex and to acquire cocaine. Legebokoff's life was quickly spiraling out of control, but he was able to keep his problems concealed from his friends and family.

Concealment of their crimes is perhaps the main trait that all serial killers share.

A Teenage Killer

At some point during Legebokoff's months-long drug binges, he decided to start killing. No doubt he had murderous fantasies for some time before doing his first kill, possibly since childhood, but it's a big step to go from thinking about murder to actually doing it.

Corey Legebokoff started his killing spree on the evening of October 9, 2009, at just the age of nineteen.

On the night in question, Legebokoff drove to Prince George's skid row and picked up some cocaine and a prostitute named Jill Stacey Stuchenko. Stuchenko was a thirty-five-year-old mother of five who was down on her luck, fighting a severe cocaine addiction. Unable to care for her children due to her addiction, Stuchenko took to the streets doing tricks to feed her expensive cocaine habit.

It is unknown if Stuchenko and Legebokoff knew each other before October 9th, but it was certainly the last time the two met. After picking up Stuchenko, the two went to a remote location on the edge of town near a gravel pit and did cocaine in Legebokoff's truck before having sex. It's not known if Legebokoff planned to kill Stuchenko, or if he snapped for some reason, but at some point during the encounter he began beating her.

Legebokoff beat her until she quit breathing and her face was a collapsed mess.

The police found Stuchenko's body in the gravel on October 20th. Besides the massive trauma sustained on her body, especially the face, there were signs she was sexually assaulted. Prince George has a relatively low crime rate, so the murder in itself was news, but since Stuchenko was a prostitute and drug user, her death quickly fell out of the headlines.

For his part, Legebokoff spent the first few days after the murder paranoid, but after her body was found and the police never showed up, his paranoia began to recede.

Corey went about his daily routine: working, partying, dating, and hanging out with his friends. To those who knew Legebokoff, he didn't seem any different in the period after October 9, 2009.

As much as Legebokoff may have enjoyed the act of killing, the whole situation scared him. He had never been in trouble with the law before and was not very familiar with law enforcement techniques. Despite becoming less paranoid of getting caught as time went by, he was still reluctant to kill again.

He didn't want to get caught.

It was at this point that the cowboy killer went into his "cooling off" period. The FBI's classification of a serial killer is contingent upon two major factors: the killer has to have murdered three or more people in a period where each is separated by time (in a series) and there has to be at least one "cooling off" period between murders. For many notorious serial killers, the cooling off period takes place after their first kill. For most serial killers, the cooling off period takes place not over any moral conflicts, but because the killer in question is afraid of capture.

But like with most serial killers, the urge, or the reasons to kill were stronger than his desire to not get caught. Legebokoff even reasoned, how would he get caught for killing prostitutes?

The urge to kill manifested itself once more in Legebokoff's soul nearly a year later. On the evening of August 31, 2010, he met another drug addict and prostitute named Natasha Lynn Montgomery.

Legebokoff is believed to have dispatched Montgomery by beating her to death in much the same way as he did Stuchenko, but he changed his method of operation a bit by disposing of her at some, as of yet, unknown location. The authorities believe that Lebegokoff dismembered Montgomery's corpse in some remote, forested location and then scattered her remains for the animals to eat.

After killing Montgomery, Legebokoff appeared to have hit his murderous groove.

Less than two weeks later, on September 10th, the cowboy killer struck again.

The victim this time was another known prostitute with a drug problem – thirty-five-year-old Cynthia Frances Maas. The cowboy killer approached Maas like all of his other victims – as a potential john and drug user – and after winning her confidence, he raped and beat her to death.

Maas was reported missing by her family, but because she was a known prostitute and drug user, they were told she was probably intentionally trying to avoid them. Cynthia's family continued to pressure the local police, until about a month after she went missing, her body was discovered in a local Prince George park.

An autopsy revealed that Maas had been raped and beaten to death with the fatal injuries coming from what appeared to be stomps to her head. The examination also showed that she had been dead for about a month.

The discovery led to immediate panic and controversy in the northern British Columbia city.

Maas' family believed that as an American Indian, she was the victim of racism. They argued that if she had been white, then the police would have done more to find her. The local police denied the accusations and pointed out that she lived a risky lifestyle and that they had no reason to believe she had been abducted or murdered when she was reported missing.

As the Maas family publicly sparred with the local police over their treatment of the case, many local residents believed that Cynthia was a victim of the enigmatic "Highway of Tears" serial killer.

The Highway of Tears refers to British Columbia Highway 16, which east to west across the northern part of the province, running through Prince George. There have been at least twenty-one murders committed along, or the victim was taken from, Highway 16 since 1969. Most Canadians are familiar with the macabre history of the highway, but there is no evidence to suggest that all, or even most, of the murders are connected. Still, many people in northern British Columbia were convinced that Maas was the killer, or killers, most recent victim.

The local, provincial, and federal law enforcement officials all looked into the theory, but few believed that Maas' death was the result of a Highway 16 serial killer. In fact, the local police seemed to rule out any serial killer and they never considered if Maas' murder was connected to Stuchenko's, or Natasha Montgomery's disappearance.

Meanwhile, the country boy killer was living the good life, attending parties and dating young women. It seemed as though Legebokoff would never be caught, but then he made a critical mistake by deviating from his m.o. and victimology.

Up until late November 2010, Legebokoff had focused most of his murderous desires on prostitutes. Homeless people, drug addicts and prostitutes are often the favored victims of serial killers because they are, in effect, invisible to polite society and people often forget about them when they go missing. Although the discovery of Legebokoff's third victim garnered media attention because her family got involved, when a suspect was not quickly found, the case receded in importance to law enforcement and the local media.

Why the cowboy killer changed his m.o. and victimology remains a mystery, but there is a good chance that hubris played a role. Since he had gotten away with three murders without anyone even vaguely thinking he was the perpetrator, there is a good chance that Legebokoff decided to up the ante by committing a more daring murder.

For his next victim, the cowboy killer went to the internet.

Legebokoff began trolling for his next victim on the Canadian social networking website Nexopia. After searching some profiles, he decided to focus on fifteen-year-old Loren Leslie. Although, Leslie was different than Legebokoff's other victims, in that she wasn't a prostitute and was a juvenile, she did have a host of problems. Leslie was on bad terms with her parents and often skipped school to hang out with her friends, drinking alcohol and smoking marijuana. The more her parents tried to discipline her, the more she rebelled.

In November of 2010, she met an attractive twenty-year-old guy on Nexopia who described himself as a country boy with a big heart. Of course, the country boy was Corey Legebokoff and about the only things truthful on his profile were his picture and his professed love of country music.

But a fifteen-year-old girl can be easily influenced by an older guy, an adult, who listens to her. After talking on-line and via text message for a few weeks, the two finally decided to take the relationship to the next level and meet in person on November 27, 2010.

It is unknown if Legebokoff immediately pounced on Loren, but it is certain that he planned to kill her. After raping and murdering the teenager, the cowboy killer took her corpse to a remote location off a logging road several miles outside of Prince George. Legebokoff must not thought much of the digital trail he left behind luring Loren into his trap, but in the end, it didn't matter anyway.

The cowboy killer took his time dismembering Leslie, as the act was all part of what drove the serial killer. Like Dahmer before him, Legebokoff was aroused, not just by the act of murder, but also when he eviscerated his victims' corpses. Once he was done cutting up the body, he spread the parts around the forest for the animals to eat.

Nature would eliminate all evidence.

But the cowboy killer was young, unsophisticated as a criminal, and a bit arrogant. Although he obviously brought Loren Leslie to the remote location to dispose of her body in a most messy way, he didn't think to bring a clean change of clothing.

As he pulled out from the logging road onto the main highway, he did so in an erratic manner that piqued the interest of a Royal Canadian Mounted Police officer who just happened to be patrolling the relatively deserted road. The officer pulled Legebokoff's truck over thinking he had a drunk driver on his hands.

A quick look at Legebokoff and the interior of the truck revealed a large amount of blood. Based on Legebokoff's demographic and the region, the officer thought that he had busted a poacher, which Legebokoff seemed to confirm. When the officer asked the cowboy killer where the carcass of the game was, though, he suddenly became less talkative.

The officer also didn't notice any meat in the back of Legebokoff's truck.

Within an hour, conservation officers arrived to check the wooded area around the logging trail, but instead of finding deer carcasses they found human limbs and a female torso.

Through a chance traffic stop, the police had just arrested a notorious serial killer

The Cowboy Killer Goes on Trial

When Legebokoff was placed in jail and charged with first-degree murder in the death of Loren Leslie, the local detectives were not only shocked at the depravity of the crime, but also by the seemingly wholesome exterior of the killer. Legebokoff did not jibe with their stereotype of a serial killer: he was young, handsome, charming, and successful.

But then the detectives were reminded of Ted Bundy.

Once the detectives realized that Legebokoff was a genuine sociopath, they took another look at some unsolved murders and disappearances around Prince George. The more they looked the more Legobokoff looked good for the murders of Jill Stuchenko, Natasha Montgomery, and Cynthia Maas in addition to Loren Leslie.

As the pre-trial maneuvering was taking place by both sides, Legebokoff tried to plead guilty to second-degree murder by admitting to be at the scene of every murder but not actually taking part in any of the violence.

Of course, the argument is ridiculous at face value. The odds that someone will ever witness a murder are fairly remote, but four times is nearly impossible. No one believed Legebokoff's story and he was squarely rebuked by the prosecutor.

"If you choose to assist that person to complete his plan, you have made yourself a party to a planned and deliberate murder," prosecutor Joseph Temple said.

With no plea bargain offered, the country boy killer was forced to go to trial, where he was found guilty on four counts of first-degree murder on September 11, 2014.

The judge handed Legebokoff a sentence of twenty-five years to life and the requirement that he be registered a sex offender for the remainder of his life. Before sending the country boy killer to serve his sentence, though, the judge had harsh words for the teen killer.

"He lacks any shred of empathy or remorse," British Columbia Supreme Court Justice Glen Parrett said of Cody Legebokoff. "He should never be allowed to walk among us again."

CHAPTER 10:
The Murder of Robbie Middleton

The problem of youth violence has been profiled throughout this book and is in many ways this volume's theme. As discussed throughout the book, the motivations for youth violence cover a wide spectrum, with the most notorious cases being driven either by unknown reasons or a thrill kill. Although all of the details of these cases diverge, most share a commonality in that the crimes that made these young people famous, or infamous, were usually single events. Yes, many of these kids had problems that led up to their extreme acts of violence, but their infamous acts were usually the culmination of whatever things were going wrong inside their heads.

There may have been warning signs, but nothing was so apparent and none had histories of committing extreme acts of violence on other kids.

The case of Robbie Middleton is different in that respect.

On the afternoon of June 28, 1998, Robbie Middleton was enjoying his eighth birthday in the woods near his family's home when he was set upon by a predator, beaten, tied to a tree, and then set on fire. Although Robbie lived through the ordeal, he suffered third-degree burns to 99% of his body leaving him permanently disfigured. Ultimately, at the age of twenty-one, Robbie died from a rare form of cancer that was the result of the many operations and skin grafts he had to endure.

The case was truly tragic on those facts alone, but it became even more so when it was revealed that the assailant was a thirteen-year-old neighborhood boy. But unlike some of the cases profiled in this book, the assault of Robbie Middleton was not this teen's first rodeo with the law. By the time Robbie's attacker reached the age of eighteen, he had committed dozens of major crimes ranging from property theft to sexual assault.

The case of Robbie Middleton has brought up the age-old question once more: are some people born evil? After reading about this case, you will probably answer yes.

The Assault

When Robbie Middleton woke up on June 28, 1998, he was all smiles. The sun was shining, school was out of session, and it was his eighth birthday: what could be better for a kid? The plan was for Robbie to spend time with his mother later that afternoon when she got home from work, but the morning and afternoon were his to do as he liked, as long as he stayed around the neighborhood.

Although Robbie was young, the Middletons lived in a quiet, safe neighborhood in the quiet, safe town of Splendora, Texas. Besides, there were always other kids in the neighborhood to play with and the adults always looked out for trouble.

But unfortunately, the trouble they usually looked for was in the form of other adults.

As Robbie was running about the woods near his house, he was suddenly grabbed and beaten. Before he had a chance to scream or run away, his attacker tied him to a tree and tormented him for a few minutes before spraying gasoline on him.

Robbie pleaded for his tormentor to let him go, but the evil person just laughed and lit Robbie on fire.

Somehow, as Robbie was engulfed in flames, he was able to wiggle free from the rope and roll on the ground to put out the fire. He then ran for blocks until he nearly made it home, collapsing on the sidewalk.

A neighbor noticed Robbie and called the ambulance.

A Long Recovery

When Robbie was brought in to the emergency room, the attending physicians didn't give him much chance of living. They told Robbie's mother that most adults wouldn't live after having 90% of their body burned and so they didn't think an eight-year-old could last very long. They told Robbie's mother to prepare for the worst.

But Robbie had a will to live that may have surprised the doctors and nurses, but it wasn't a surprise to his family.

Robbie survived the initial operations and the first few weeks in critical condition, but he faced the daunting task of years of therapy and recovery. Ultimately, he needed over 150 operations, many of which were painful skin grafts. Still, Robbie faced the future with a good attitude and rarely complained about the chronic pain.

When Robbie's condition stabilized, the local police visited him in order to find out what exactly happened. Since he was so young and playing unattended, the police thought that he could have accidentally burned himself or possibly he was burned playing with fire with some other kids.

The police were shocked to learn that it was no accident.

Robbie named thirteen-year-old neighborhood boy Don Wilburn Collins as his attacker, but offered no motive.

And the police refused to press the disfigured eight-year-old for further information.

The police arrested Collins for felony aggravated assault and placed him in a juvenile facility to await trial. After sitting in the facility for several months, a judge decided to release Collins, stating that beyond Middleton's hospital room accusation, there was no evidence tying the boy to the assault.

The police knew that Robbie wasn't lying, but there was little they

114

could do. They had to fall back on good old-fashioned detective work in order to bring the twisted teen to justice.

Meanwhile, Robbie tried to move on with his life. Besides the countless operations and skin grafts that he had to endure and the fact that his face was permanently disfigured, Robbie wanted to attend normal schools. Although he had to deal with plenty of stares and some cruel jokes, Robbie persisted and eventually developed a network of friends who were loyal to him throughout his high school years.

Robbie did well in his classes and by his senior year, was one of the most popular kids in his class. But his medical problems continued to be an albatross around his neck. Just when things would seem to be going well for Robbie in school or socially, he would have to leave school temporarily for a series of more operations. Most of Robbie's operations were done in various Shriner's hospitals around the country, which is where he met other kids in situations similar to his, some worse.

Robbie used his time spent in hospitals constructively, by making contacts with doctors and others who specialized in helping burn victims. He learned about the medical procedures, the costs, and how indigent people can or cannot afford to pay for the treatments.

Eventually, Robbie took his knowledge and experience as a burn victim and became an advocate for others in his situation. He gave talks about the subject at hospitals around the country and became the face of a movement that advocated for more funds to research burn treatments and procedures.

Truly, Robbie had turned the awful circumstances of his life into a testament to human resiliency, helping others in the process.

Still, something was missing – justice.

Years had gone by and the only suspect in Robbie's assault, Don Collins, had yet to receive any justice for his heinous act. And as time went by, it became painfully clear that Don Collins was the type of person born to do bad things and would continue to do so until he was put away for a long time.

Don Collins

The term bully has been used quite frequently in recent years and some would say overused. Bullies come in all shapes and sizes but share one thing in common: they get pleasure from seeing fear in others. The average schoolyard bully may use violence, or the threat of violence, to intimidate his victims, but often enough many bullies turn out to be more bite than bark.

There was definitely bite behind Don Collins' bark.

By the age of thirteen, Don Collins had already made a reputation for himself in Splendora as a budding thug and bully.

But Collins took his bullying beyond just teasing, words, or even threats.

Collins routinely beat neighborhood kids younger and smaller than him and when there wasn't a kid around for him to abuse, he turned his wrath on animals.

"Everyone was afraid of him. He was the big bully that stomped kittens to death," said Robbie's mom, Colleen.

And by "everyone," Colleen even meant the adults in the area. Collins had no guidance at home and the other adults in the neighborhood were afraid to say anything for fear of what he might do. He was frequently seen carrying knives, clubs, and other weapons and was known to have an unnatural attraction to fire.

Robbie Middleton unfortunately learned about Collins' love of fire the hard way.

After Collins was released from the juvenile hall due to a lack of evidence in the fire borne assault on Robbie Middleton, the adults of the neighborhood grew even more afraid of the Romanesque child living among them. Parents kept their eyes on their children more, but they weren't able to keep an eye on them, or Collins, all the time.

Don Collins struck again in 2001.

About three years after he attacked Robbie, at the age of sixteen, Collins attacked another eight-year-old boy in Splendora. The attack was eerily similar to the one on Robbie in many ways. He singled out an unsuspecting boy who appeared to be alone, pulled a gun, and then sexually assaulted the boy. Unlike the attack on

Middleton, though, justice caught up to Collins the second time.

Collins was arrested and charged with felony assault and battery and felony sexual assault and remanded to a juvenile facility to await trial. Although the details of the case are sealed because privacy laws regarding juvenile defendants in the United States, it is known that Collins served four years in a Texas juvenile facility for the crime.

Texas is known for its tough adult prisons, but the juvenile facilities also have acquired somewhat of a violent reputation. Many of the same gangs present in the adult facilities have a presence in the juvenile camps and assaults are not uncommon in some of the more tougher units. Generally speaking, the bigger kids, known gang members, and bullies, such as Collins, are separated from the younger and weaker kids, but that still doesn't stop all the violence.

Despite the sometimes rough nature of Texas' juvenile corrections system, the officials do emphasize rehabilitation, as every kid in the system will be released into society one day. Vocational and treatment programs were available for Collins to take part in while he was incarcerated, but instead of working to better himself and atone for the pain he had caused others, Collins appeared to have been merely counting the days until he was released.

Once he was released, although convicted of the crime as a juvenile, Collins was required to register as a sex offender as an adult. But instead of following the rules, Collins quickly disappeared and decided to do things his own way, doing drugs and committing more crimes.

Eventually, Collins was arrested, charged, and convicted of failing to register as a sex offender. He was sent to the adult department of corrections and released in 2011.

While Collins was serving time in adult prison, the authorities of Splendora and Montgomery County began looking at him as a potential suspect in some unsolved cases. The cases included burglaries, sexual assaults, and arsons, but one case kept surfacing to the top – the assault of Robbie Middleton.

The Montgomery County prosecutors wanted to get justice for Robbie and his mother and wanted to make sure that Collins would never be able to victimize another child.

Charges Filed

As Collins spent the 2000s partying and victimizing people, Robbie Middleton was fighting for his life. Although he was brave and strong for his age, the injuries he suffered in the 1998 attack were just too much for a human, especially one so young, to handle. Finally, after fighting most of his life, Robbie Middleton died of a rare form of cancer in 2011, just months before his twenty-first birthday.

The news was of course devastating to those who knew Robbie, but something positive came out of it – a way to finally arrest

Collins. Two weeks before he died, Robbie gave a videotaped statement where he said that Collins had raped him two weeks before the fire attack.

"He pulled my clothes down and started raping me," Middleton said on his deathbed.

The Montgomery County prosecutors thought that Robbie's confession, along with Collins' m.o. of sexually assaulting young boys, was enough to bring charges. But the prosecutors were not content to charge Collins with assault; they charged him with murder based on the testimony of Middleton's doctors who said the cancer was the result of operations, which only happened because he was so thoroughly burned.

Don Collins was arrested and charged with first-degree murder as an adult in the death of Robbie Middleton in 2013.

When Collins finally went to trial in 2015, he denied having anything to do with the 1998 assault. His lawyers argued that since no one saw him commit the crime, then there was not enough evidence to convict. The defense may have worked for a less odious individual, but the judge allowed witnesses from the neighborhood to testify about Collins' egregious behavior toward other children, animals, and even adults.

Needless to say, the jury did not find Collins sympathetic.

Collins was convicted of first-degree murder and sentenced to forty years in the Texas Department of Corrections. Based on the nature of Texas' correctional system, it is very unlikely that Collins will serve all of that time behind bars.

Despite the long sentence and a conviction for killing a child, Collins was unperturbed by the entire affair.

"The bright side of this is I'll come out with an education," Collins was heard saying to one of his attorneys.

Collins is correct, he does have a good chance of getting educated in one of Texas' tougher prisons where he will no doubt be sent. Since his case was well-publicized, all of the seasoned convicts and gang members will know just how sick Collins' crimes are and many will likely want to teach him a thing or two.

Don Collins' education may end up being about how child predators are treated in American prisons.

CHAPTER 11:
The Portland Machete Murder

One of the major problems that modern, industrialized criminal justice systems face is how to deal with mentally ill criminals. The reality is that a sizable amount of any population is afflicted with varying forms of mental illness at any time and although most of those people lead productive, normal lives, for some the illness proves too much.

For those with the worst forms of mental illness, round the clock care and a very specific medicine regime are needed to keep the diseases in check. Sometimes it is all too much, which leads to the afflicted person living on the streets. Statistics vary concerning what percentage of the homeless suffer from mental illness, but all studies show it is several times higher than average. On the streets, the mentally ill are forced to live on the charity of others and if that is not enough they turn to crime.

Although rare, sometimes the crimes they commit are quite violent.

Erik Meiser

Erik Meiser was born in the mid-1970s and as soon as he could talk, people knew there was something wrong with him. He suffered from hallucinations and delusions at an early age, which resulted in him being hospitalized and diagnosed with schizophrenia.

Although Meiser's childhood was difficult, he lived a pretty normal life in his early adulthood thanks to a regular antipsychotic medicine regime. Eventually, he was able to find steady employment and even started a family, but the problems of schizophrenia were never far away. By the late 1990s, Meiser would quit taking his meds for long periods of time, which would result in him having hallucinations and paranoid episodes. Because of that, he was unable to keep steady employment and began drifting from job to job and town to town.

When Meiser was off his prescribed meds, he would try to substitute by self-medicating with alcohol or illicit drugs, particularly cocaine and methamphetamine. The latter two drugs proved to be especially harmful, as they raised his paranoia to a level that his family thought was unimaginable. When he did visit his family, it was to tell them about a shadowy conspiracy against him. Since Meiser's family was well-acquainted with his condition, they tried not to indulge his ideas but things got worse.

Meiser believed that there was not only a shadowy conspiracy of people out to get him, but that they were trying to turn his son into a cannibal.

By the late 2000s, Meiser's family heard little from him. The schizophrenic father spent most of his time hiding from the shadowy conspiracy and to make ends meet, he would burglarize homes throughout the state of Oregon.

Erik Meiser had an uncanny aptitude for burglary.

The Machete Attack

In September 2012, Erik Meiser was having a difficult time. He had been homeless again for several months and was off his antipsychotic medication, so he was feeling especially paranoid. He thought that a cannibal cult was following him throughout the state of Oregon and that at any moment they could capture him and eat him alive.

During this period, Meiser spent most of his time on the streets of Portland, burglarizing homes to get money for his next meth fix. On one pleasant late summer evening, Meiser was scoping out a Portland neighborhood and ended up at the home of Fritz Hayes Junior and his wife Margaret.

Meiser noticed that most of the lights were off, so he crept up slowly to the back of the house.

After looking in a number of the windows and not seeing any movement, Meiser reached into his trusty bag and pulled out a crowbar and hammer, which he used to gain entry into the home through the back door.

Like a career burglar, Meiser went past the expensive electronic items and went straight to the bedrooms. He could always grab whatever electronic items he could fit into his bag on the way out, but first he needed to locate the more valuable items such as cash and jewelry. As Meiser was rifling through the couple's bedroom, he heard something in the front of the house.

Did the cannibal cult find him?

Fritz and Margaret were a young couple who liked to spend their money on each other whenever possible. On the night in question, Fritz surprised his wife with a dinner date at an expensive local restaurant. After their meal, the couple drove back to their home and immediately noticed that a light was on in their bedroom.

Fritz told Margaret to wait in the driveway.

As soon as Fritz entered the home, he was attacked by Meiser, who had a machete.

Meiser was hacking away at Fritz, who managed to fight off the crazed the attacker to a certain extent. The attack ended up on the Hayes' front lawn, which is where Meiser finally got the upper hand. The crazed impulses of the schizophrenic, combined with the machete were just too much for Hayes, who died on his front lawn from multiple machete hacks.

Immediately after killing Hayes, Meiser fled the neighborhood. He knew that he had just killed someone, but he wasn't sure who the person was. Meiser began to think that Hayes was actually part of the cannibal cult and that it would only be a matter of time before they found him among the sizable homeless population of Portland.

Meiser had to flee the area.

When the police showed up at the Hayes home to investigate the attack, they had little to go on. They knew the attacker was a white male, but they didn't have much else. Since the crime happened in an otherwise quiet neighborhood, it garnered considerable local media attention, which is where the first tip came to the police.

A random tip to the police said that the assailant was probably a man named Erik Meiser and that he was hiding in the southern Oregon town of Corvallis.

Within days, the Corvallis Police arrested Meiser and he was brought back to Portland to stand trial in Multnomah County for the first-degree murder of Fritz Hayes Junior.

This would turn out to be a case that proves sometimes the wheels of justice turn slowly.

Years of Legal Proceedings

When Erik Meiser was brought before a judge for his initial bond hearing, it was apparent that he suffered from mental illness. A review of his medical and criminal records revealed that, in fact,

Meiser had spent a good part of his life in mental institutions and correctional facilities.

Meiser's attorneys decided to present an insanity defense.

Although Meiser's mental illness was well-documented and it no doubt contributed to Hayes' murder, it was also a fact that he willfully quit taking his antipsychotic medications. It was also a fact that he self-medicated with illicit drugs and alcohol, even though he knew the negative side effects of doing so. In other words, there were numerous factors that worked against Meiser beating the case by way of insanity.

And it is not like he would necessarily beat the case that way, anyway. If found not guilty by reason of insanity, he would probably be confined to a secured mental hospital for the rest of his life.

Still, his attorneys fought on and on in what seemed like endless hearings to determine Meiser's mental ability to stand trial.

Meiser was declared unfit to stand trial three times, but was eventually cleared by a judge and stood trial in 2017, more than five years after Hayes was murdered. Meiser was convicted of first-degree murder and sentenced to twenty-five years to life in prison.

Recognizing that mental illness played a role in the murder, the judge ruled that Meiser would begin his sentence for an indeterminate amount of years in a mental hospital.

Hopefully, for the sake of the staff and inmates at the facility, Meiser no longer thinks that a cannibal cult is after him.

CHAPTER 12:
The Murder of Cassie Jo Stoddart

The final case profiled in this volume is yet another brutal example of youth crime. Although the details of this crime are certainly shocking, the legal repercussions are far more important.

We all know that youth crime is a problem in the United States and that it causes tremendous damage to society. The victims of youth crime are of course the ones most obviously affected. Youth property crimes cost millions of dollars a year and as costly as that is, it is nearly impossible to put a price tag on the amount of damage that youth violence has brought to countless innocent victims. No one will argue that youth crime has been extremely costly to the United States.

What people will argue, though, is how to deal with youth offenders. Correctional philosophies, like many things, tend to be cyclical. Youth criminals were once treated fairly lightly in this country: as an example, until the 1980s, it was extremely rare for juvenile offenders, even those charged with murder, to be certified as adults. Since the 1980s, it has become regular practice in many states to charge juveniles above the age of fifteen, especially repeat offenders, with felonies in the adult court system for a variety of different crimes. Rehabilitation is still stressed to a certain degree, but the philosophy is now that it must be accompanied with stiff repercussions.

But what about juvenile murderers?

When the crime rate peaked in the United States in the early 1980s, juvenile crime actually went up, which included the taboo crime of homicide.

The courts were left to figure out what to do with a vast increase of homicidal teenagers. The reality is that juvenile killers, like killers in general, had little sympathy from the American public in general. Most Americans were fine with giving juvenile killers life sentences, or even the death penalty. By the late 2000s, there were up to 1,800 men and women serving life sentences in American prisons who committed their crimes as juveniles.

State and federal legislatures followed the public sentiment concerning this specific class of killers by giving them little attention. But the courts are a separate government branch in the United States and quite capable of changing things in their own right.

The next case is one in where an example of brutal teen violence became famous, not so much for the details of the case, but more so for the legal challenges that followed.

Unexpected Violence

Pocatello, Idaho is a small but growing city in the state's southeastern agricultural region. The city is home to Idaho State University and within a short drive to the more scenic and mountainous areas of the state. Unemployment and crime are low and the air is clean, which has made Pocatello a magnet for migrants seeking to escape the crime, high taxes, and overcrowding of California.

Cassie Jo Stoddart's family were among those who left California to escape its problems, but unfortunately they learned that the phenomenon of youth violence can happen anywhere, at any time.

On the evening of September 22, 2006, sixteen-year-old Cassie was housesitting with her boyfriend in a quiet Pocatello neighborhood. As they began the evening by watching some movies, the doorbell rang. Standing on the porch were their two sixteen-year-old friends, Brian Lee Draper and Torey Michael Adamick. Cassie invited the two boys inside and the four sat down to watch some movies.

Draper and Adamick hadn't known Cassie very long at that point, but the three shared a mutual friend in Cassie's boyfriend. Cassie liked Draper and Adamick, although she admitted to other friends that the two could be weird at times and liked to talk about violence. Writing it off as typical testosterone teenage talk, Cassie often invited the two along when she was with her boyfriend.

Adamick and Draper were not the type of boys who stood out in the crowd. They both looked fairly average and neither did anything to attract attention. They were just two anonymous kids in Pocatello.

But Draper and Adamick didn't want to be anonymous. They wanted everyone to know their names.

As the four watched television for a while, Draper and Adamick told Cassie and her boyfriend that they changed their minds and decided to go to a movie theater. They said their goodbyes and left. Shortly after Draper and Adamick left, Cassie's boyfriend also left in time to make his curfew.

Minutes after Cassie's boyfriend left the house, the power went out. Before Cassie could even check the circuit breaker, she was set upon by Draper and Adamick. The two boys took turns with one holding Cassie down while the other stabbed her.

The coroner's report indicated that Cassie was stabbed a total of twenty-nine times.

The news horrified the quiet Idaho city and a manhunt ensued to find the killer of the innocent teenager. At first, the local police believed that the perpetrator was probably a well-seasoned criminal, such as a burglar or sex-offender.

But their theory quickly changed when they put together a chronology of Cassie's last hours.

Since Cassie's boyfriend, Brian Draper, and Torey Adamick were the last ones to see Cassie alive, they were all brought in for questioning as suspects. Cassie's boyfriend was quickly cleared, but once the police put a little pressure on the other two, they quickly cracked. The boys both admitted to taking part in the murder, but they also tried to mitigate their guilt by pointing the finger at the other. When the investigators asked why they killed someone who was supposed to be their friend, they answered in vague terms about being influenced by horror movies and the 1999 Columbine massacre.

It was an open and shut case against the two. They were both found guilty of first-degree murder and sentenced to life without the chance of parole in 2007.

But in many ways the case was just getting started.

Miller v. Alabama

As stated above, the movement to treat juvenile criminals more lightly, or as their advocates would say, "more humanely," has in recent years moved from the legislative branch to the judicial branch. Attorneys in the prison reform movement believed that they could successfully challenge life sentences without the possibility of parole for juveniles under the Eighth Amendment of the United States Constitution, which forbids the use of "cruel and unusual punishment."

Although the strategy had been tried unsuccessfully, a case involving a fourteen-year-old boy who had been convicted of murder in Alabama and given a life sentence came before the United States Supreme Court in 2012.

In a five to four ruling, the Supreme Court ruled in *Miller v. Alabama* that it was unconstitutional to impose a mandatory life sentence on a juvenile, even those convicted of murder. It does not mean that a juvenile *cannot* be given a life sentence, only that the judge must consider the defendants age before passing sentence.

As big as this ruling was, it did little to help Draper and Adamick. They were stuck in the Idaho Department of Corrections doing their mandatory life sentences. It might have mattered if they had committed their murder six years later, but it did little to help them.

But then came another ruling in 2016.

The Supreme Court ruled in *Montgomery v. Louisiana* that *Miller v. Alabama* should be applied retroactively. The ruling immediately affected over 2,000 people in American prisons, including Draper and Adamick.

As of the time this was written, the two have filed petitions to be resentenced but are awaiting the court's decision.

Conclusion

After reading this book, you may view crime a bit differently. Instead of seeing crime as something that happens to other people on the other side of town, it is evident that violent crimes comes in many different forms and is perpetrated by a wide range of people.

Many of them children.

The problem of youth violence, like all crime generally, will probably never be totally eradicated, but perhaps some day soon, our society will learn more about what drives this phenomenon. Unfortunately, when viewing the many examples of youth crime profiled in this book, the prognosis does not look good. Until society completely understands what drives youth violence, it can not be alleviated and as this book has shown, there are many reasons why kids kill.

Sometimes kids kill for no reason at all.

This volume also sheds light on many bizarre crimes, some of them perpetrated by juveniles. As difficult as it is for any well-adjusted, law-abiding person to contemplate crime in general, some of the crimes profiled in this book would make a career criminal sick.

Crime is certainly a sickness that afflicts society and like biological diseases, it will be impossible to eradicate it all, but perhaps trying to understand the worst cases will be a start.

More books by Jack Rosewood

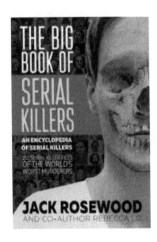

There is little more terrifying than those who hunt, stalk, and snatch their prey under the cloak of darkness. These hunters search not for animals, but for the touch, taste, and empowerment of human flesh. They are cannibals, vampires, and monsters, and they walk among us.

These serial killers are not mythical beasts with horns and shaggy hair. They are people living among society, going about their day to day activities until nightfall. They are the Dennis Rader's, the fathers, husbands, church-going members of the community.

This A-Z encyclopedia of 150 serial killers is the ideal reference book. Included are the most famous true crime serial killers, like Jeffrey Dahmer, John Wayne Gacy, and Richard Ramirez, not to mention the women who kill, such as Aileen Wuornos and

Martha Rendell. There are also lesser-known serial killers covering many countries around the world, so the range is broad.

Each of the serial killer files includes information on when and how they killed the victims, the background of each killer, or the suspects in some cases, such as the Zodiac killer, their trials and punishments. For some, there are chilling quotes by the killers themselves. The Big Book of Serial Killers is an easy to follow collection of information on the world's most heinous murderers.

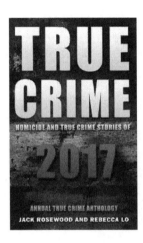

Every year, we look back in horror at the sheer evil mankind is capable of, and 2017 was no different.

Across the world, but particularly in the United States, startlingly horrific crimes have almost become commonplace, causing us to double-lock our doors at night and look over our shoulders, wondering if we're safe, no matter how crowded or well-lit our location is.

In this true crime release, we've compiled some of the most gripping and gruesome crime stories of 2017. Some of the horrible stories you will read about includes:

- A Florida serial killer stalked a close-knit suburb of Tampa, killing Seminole Heights residents seemingly at random.
- A member of a neo-Nazi organization used his vehicle to kill a protestor in Charlottesville, Virginia, more than 50 years after the world defeated Hitler's racist rise to power.
- A couple was sentenced to death for brutalizing a 10-year-old girl for years, beating her, depriving her of food, forcing

her to walk on the hot pavement of a sizzling summer in Arizona, only to let her die in an airtight box overnight, her punishment for eating a Popsicle without asking after sweltering in 115-degree heat.

- Two young girls were smart enough to record pictures and audio of a man suspected in their deaths, evidence that will hopefully soon solve their murders.
- A blood-soaked man carried his mother's decapitated head into a grocery store, attacking a clerk and stabbing him as well before being apprehended from police.
- The UK was rocked by terrorist bombings that turned joyous moments deadly in an instant.
- The death of Charles Manson gave us an opportunity to look back at the bloody mayhem inspired by a murderous man with a messiah complex.

Keep the lights on, Dear Reader, and welcome to 2017's most horrifying true stories.

There are reasons why some of the most famous serial killers in the world have names that stick in our memories, send shivers up our spines, make us double-check to make sure the doors are locked at night, and maybe peek under the bed to be sure nothing is lurking there before we turn off the lights.

These are monsters who are real, whose crimes are so reprehensible, so horrific, that they become seared in our memories.

For this true crime anthology, we've combed the serial killer files to give you a closer, more intimate look at some of the worst of the worst from the world of serial killers, combining multiple stories into one perfect late-night read that's just the thing to keep you up at night, unable to stop turning the pages.

For those who love criminology, who can't put down the latest true crime stories, this collection of stories rivals the best serial killer books, and give you deeper insight into killers ranging from the charismatic, cunning Ted Bundy to the long-abused Aileen

Wuornos, whose unimaginable troubles finally came to a very violent head.

This diverse collection of serial killer stories, culled from the annals of history, is an ideal choice for the true crime buff who wonders why the monsters of our imaginations came to life and walked the streets, lurking in dark corners to wait for their next victim.

GET THESE BOOKS FOR FREE

Go to http://www.jackrosewood.com/free

and get these E-Books for free!

A Note from the Author

Hello, this is Jack Rosewood. Thank you for reading this book. I hope you enjoyed the read. If you did, I'd appreciate if you would take a few moments to **post a review on Amazon.**

I would also love if you'd sign up to my newsletter to receive updates on new releases, promotions, and a FREE copy of my Herbert Mullin E-Book, www.JackRosewood.com

Thanks again for reading this book, make sure to follow me on Facebook.

Best Regards

Jack Rosewood

94634265R00085

Made in the USA
Columbia, SC
27 April 2018